SERVICE MOST SILENT

By the same author

The Bader Wing*
VCs of the Royal Navy
Prisoner at Large
Hovering Angels
Periscope Patrol
Invasion '44
VCs of the Air
Battle Stations
Highly Explosive
The Blinding Flash
VCs of the Army
A Girl called Johnnie
Famous Air Battles
Destination Berchtesgaden
British Aircraft of World War 2
Famous Flights
VCs of the Second World War*
For Gallantry – Awards of the George Cross 1940 – 2005*
The Life and Selected Works of Rupert Brooke*
Heroic Flights*
The Good Spy Guide
The Yanks are Coming
Fight for the Sea
Fight for the Air
The Bader Tapes
The Battle of Britain
Frank Sinatra

special research credited in
Fight for the Sky *by Douglas Bader**

**In print with Pen & Sword Books Ltd*

SERVICE MOST SILENT

The Navy's Fight against Enemy Mines

by

John Frayn Turner

Pen & Sword
MARITIME

First published in Great Britain in 1955 by George G. Harrap & Co Ltd
Reprinted in this format in 2008 by
PEN & SWORD MARITIME
an imprint of
Pen & Sword Books Ltd
47 Church Street
Barnsley
South Yorkshire
S70 2AS

Copyright © John Frayn Turner, 1955, 2008

ISBN 978 1 84415 726 6

The right of John Frayn Turner to be identified as author of this
work has been asserted by him in accordance with the
Copyright, Designs and Patents Act 1988.

A CIP catalogue record for this book is
available from the British Library.

Printed and bound in Great Britain
By CPI UK

Pen & Sword Books Ltd incorporates the Imprints of
Pen & Sword Aviation, Pen & Sword Maritime,
Pen & Sword Military, Wharncliffe Local History,
Pen & Sword Select, Pen & Sword Military Classics and Leo Cooper.

For a complete list of Pen & Sword titles please contact
PEN & SWORD BOOKS LIMITED
47 Church Street, Barnsley, South Yorkshire, S70 2AS, England
E-mail: enquiries@pen-and-sword.co.uk
Website: www.pen-and-sword.co.uk

Preface

ONE day during the War, on a wild, windswept foreshore of the Outer Orkneys, two naval officers trudged slowly over the mud towards an enemy mine that lay in the wash of the incoming tide. As they approached, while they were still some way off, a wave rolled the mine over—and it exploded. The officers were injured; their wounds went untended; with no one near, they died. And the waves broke over their bodies, flattening for ever the footsteps in the sand. . . .

It is now ten years since the War was won. A decade divides us from those dramatic days. Time has flown by on jet-propelled wings, and memory become dulled of the men who mattered—and matter still. So before the years crowd them aside, and their records are finally filed, the saga must be sung of the Navy's men of the mines, who on the beaches of Britain and far foreign shores dissected the deadliest weapons the enemy could devise, so that counter-measures could be conceived, the seas swept clear, our ships saved. Our lives, too. For the Few of the Navy saved us as surely as did their name-sakes above in the air. So many are their exploits that only a cross-section can be chronicled. To those of them who died, officers and men alike, this book is dedicated.

J. F. T.

Contents

Illustrations

1

Contact

"CONSEQUENTLY this country is at war ..." Mr Chamberlain's words echoed emotionally across the drawing-room and through the open window, carrying far down the lawn till they were lost in the haze of a Hampshire landscape. A cloud moved in front of the sun; its shadow sped over the grass; a breeze shivered through the trees, stirring them out of their Sunday stupor. And all at once late summer turned to early autumn.

"What do you think it will mean, John," Lorna asked, "not just for us, but for every one?" The two boys, Robin and Philip, looked over to their father as she spoke.

John Ouvry pulled on his pipe for a moment. "We can't really know yet. We seem to have lived through nothing but scares lately, one way and another; so we'd better just wait and see."

As it happened, he did not have long to wait. The Prime Minister's voice ended. Ouvry put on his jacket, with the two and a half rings of a lieutenant-commander, and gazed out of the window, hands behind back.

The house, Somerfields, stood on ground gently declining from the country outskirts of Fareham away to the Solent, two or three miles distant. And, by a coincidence, in a straight line beyond the stretch of water lay

Osborne, in the Isle of Wight, where Ouvry had served part of his cadetship when only a little older than Robin was now. How old was the boy? Ten already? For a minute Ouvry was back at Osborne more than twenty-five years earlier, with the First War still to come. His mind moved to 1917 and his appointment as mining officer to a cruiser. Twenty-two years, on and off, he must have been looking at mines.

The phone rang, bringing him back to the unreal reality of another war.

"Commander M [Mining] here, Ouvry. Can you come down to *Vernon*? We've a lot to discuss. It looks as if we'll have all our work cut out for a while, what with trials of our own stuff and keeping an eye on the things they'll be cooking up for us. And, Ouvry "—here Commander Sayer paused, as if loath to go on—"you look like being the one most qualified to deal with any Jerry mines that may come our way sooner or later. You know that, don't you? So keep on the top line."

Exactly a week later, at 1725 on Sunday, September 10, the s.s. *Magdapur* was steaming slowly through the channel between Aldeburgh Napes and Sizewell Bank, up the East Coast a little from Harwich and Orford Ness, when a deep explosion disturbed the afternoon calm of Suffolk coastal villagers. Those who looked eastward out of their windows saw the ship sinking rapidly, her back broken and boiler burst. It was two hours after low water, and she lay in seventy feet on an even keel, with both masts showing—an eerie sight which was to be repeated all too frequently round our coasts during the following few years.

Suspicions were at once aroused, as this much used

channel north of Harwich had been properly swept for any normal horn mines with sinkers which the Germans might have been able to lay, or for similar mines that might have strayed from British defensive fields. The latter was highly unlikely, as our own minefields at that stage were to a large extent 'propaganda publications,' due to initial shortages of the actual mines and of ships with which to lay them. As the *Magdapur* was the first loss, nothing more than conjecture was possible, for she might have been sunk by torpedo from a U-boat. Further sweeps for buoyant mines were immediately ordered in the vicinity of the wreck, both by fast shallow-draught minesweepers and by converted trawlers. No mines came to light. Meanwhile there seemed little to do but wait and prepare.

Six days two hours forty-five minutes elapsed without incident—just long enough a lull to encourage a false sense of security. Then at 2010 on Saturday, September 16, an external explosion occurred to the westward of Aldeburgh Napes which severely shook the s.s. *City of Paris* as she sailed through. The state of the tide was low water; the depth fifty-two to seventy feet. Violently blasted, the ship seemed to be sinking, and was justifiably abandoned by her crew. Later, however, seeing her still afloat, they returned aboard to find her seaworthy, but with her heavy machinery damaged. Next day she managed to make port at Tilbury under her own steam, where a thorough examination revealed that *she had not been holed in any part of her hull.*

Here was the first suggestion of proof. Assuming that mines sank the *Magdapur* and damaged the *City of Paris*, at no time had they come in contact with either vessel. The ships had caused them to fire, but by some influence other than the direct hit of the old horn. The mine menace had shown itself. There was only one thing to do—find a mine, take it to bits, and see how it worked.

It was Monday the 18th, and Sayer, Commander M, had just read the signal from Tilbury. As Ouvry came into his office Sayer was clearly worried. He turned away from his window that looked on to Portsmouth Harbour. "Another ship hit near Aldeburgh, Ouvry. It looks like a magnetic or acoustic job. We could be wrong, of course; but all the signs seem to suggest it. Nothing's allowed through the channel. One convoy got through safely, but now they're being diverted. Sweeps still can't find anything."

"And I don't think they will, sir," Ouvry chipped in glumly. "There's not much we can do by remote control down here, anyway, is there?"

"No. I think the only way to tackle it is on the spot, so I want you to go up to Harwich and try and get hold of one of these damned things somehow."

By the following lunch-time, Tuesday, September 19, Ouvry was at Parkeston Quay, Harwich. Here he con-tacted Sub-Lieutenant Meikle, and together they ran through the details of a proposed plan of action. With the channel swept as near the bottom as possible—seven to eight fathoms, or forty-two to forty-eight feet—they decided on a combined operation. Despite a steady north-easterly wind, and a strong sea running, a small assorted convoy sailed at dawn on the 22nd. The plan was the best that could be devised, but as Ouvry saw the shore fading he could not help feeling an inadequacy about the whole thing. The minesweepers *Mastiff* and *Cedar* were to sweep along the bottom, up the channel between the *City of Paris* position and the wreck of the *Magdapur*. If a mine came to the surface the third sweeper, *Hussar*, carrying Ouvry and his mine-recovery party—Chief Petty Officer Baldwin, with Able Seamen Vearncombe and Boobier—was to stay near it for half an hour while Ouvry sketched and photographed it. Then, if practicable, the mine was to be enveloped in a hemp net rigged between the sweeper's two whalers and to be secured astern of the *Hussar*. If the mine could be secured *Hussar* would tow it thirty-five miles at slow speed near to a sheltered beach selected for landing, when an M.T.B. under Meikle would take over and tow it inshore, where a party was waiting to haul it up on the beach.

For ninety minutes the trio proceeded in impossible conditions, with the *Hussar* party uncomfortably placed astern of *Mastiff* and *Cedar*. No one knew what would happen if a mine were to be stirred from the depths; but, fortunately, all was comparatively quiet, save for the whine of the wind and a slashing sea. An apprehensive hour and a half, with the wreck of the *Magdapur* reminding them all the time of the worst that could happen. When Ouvry got ashore that evening a signal was waiting for him from the Admiralty saying "Abandon the search."

"How did it go?" Sayer gripped Ouvry's hand warmly. "Come in and tell me all about it."

"No can do, I'm afraid, sir—at least, not that way. Everything was against it, even if we had found one.

If we could only get to grips on some beach or other we'd soon fix it."

"You still think it's a magnetic or acoustic, or some other bright idea? Couldn't torpedoes by any chance have caused the two losses?"

"No. I'm pretty sure now that it's a case of non-contacts. Influence mines, the Americans are calling them, I hear. Rather queer, really—the thing that's made up my mind for me has nothing to do with this week's fiasco. It was that report from the coastguard at Aldeburgh which came in during August—before the War even. You remember it. A German ship was seen manœuvring near the Napes, but disappeared before she could be contacted. It seems pretty certain now that the site for an offensive minefield was being investigated and a survey of the area made. I believe Jerry laid a field the day after war broke out—probably from a merchantman steaming across the channel up there. Ground mines[1] could easily be dumped without causing suspicion—probably packed in wooden cases, knowing the Germans."

"It's pretty clear, then, that something of the sort happened, but we've still got to solve it. We've had it from high up that we must do everything possible. They realize the dangers involved, you may be sure, but are also aware of the dangerous situation this could become."

It was Sunday. Both men were looking tired and more than a bit baffled. Behind them they had the civilian brains of the Mine Design Department, and specifically its scientific section, who would be collaborating on the examination of any specimens once they were found—

[1] Influence mines lying on the bottom.

and made safe. But first they had to be found. A duty rating came into Sayer's room, cap in one hand, message in the other. "Signal from Admiralty, sir."

Sayer read it rapidly. "Well, if we had any doubts left about Aldeburgh this rounds off the story the coast-guards started in August."

He gave Ouvry a précis of the contents: "s.s. *Phryne* was sunk just to eastward of Aldeburgh Napes in eighty-one feet at 0800 this morning. Took two hours to go down. One a week-end three times running—and there's not a damn thing we can do about it."

So ended a month of war, 'phoney' to some, frustrating to *Vernon*. Then, snapping the tension, came an interlude. One morning in early October the trawler *Tokyo* was fishing off the Swarte Bank when one of her hands, Bill, was helping to haul in her trawl. Looking out to sea for relief from the job, he suddenly shouted, "My God, look at 'em—a couple of mines in the trawl!" And so there were, two spherical horned objects, one of them silver, deftly caught among a squirming mass of fish. Not surprisingly, the skipper gave the order: "Slip the trawl. We're making back to Grimsby." Admiralty ordered a search to be organized by Flag Officer, Humber, and Ouvry headed north-east again.

As at Harwich, everything seemed against the project from the word go. Ouvry got up to Hull at 1500 on Saturday, October 7. Chief Petty Officer Baldwin and his two sailors brought up the rear (and the gear) by lorry later the same day. Next morning Baldwin reported to Ouvry. "I'm as happy about this plan as I was with the last shot, Chief," Ouvry volunteered. "These are the orders, anyway. We can but try. It's another

B

eternal triangle: two trawlers (they've never swept before!) are going to try to get a mine; we'll be in the third to recover it."

"Sounds all right in theory, sir," said Baldwin, eyeing the rain lashing against the window-panes of the little office.

"I know what you're thinking, Chief, and I share your sentiments entirely, but we've got to go through with it —or at least give it a try."

Ouvry was visualizing the prospect of sailing out at dawn in weather too rough for fishing, and wrestling with a strange mine swinging inboard, while feeling very sick in the stomach—he was no small-ship sailor—and then undoing the blessed thing in a swell incited by an easterly wind which was now reaching gale force. This grappling with intangibles was beginning to get him down. He was a sensitive, modest man, with a level voice and head, who saw his duty quite clearly and looked on it as just that—no more. Here was his particular part to play, and he would feel fully confident to do so—given reasonable conditions. But this hopeless, haphazard quest was different. He went ahead, nevertheless, with all the determination associated with aquiline features.

As the trawlers operated from Grimsby, he transferred his party there, and reported to the Naval Officer in Charge. "Glad to see you, Ouvry." N.O.I.C.'s words were welcoming, at any rate. "So you're going out for a mine? Which colour do you want? We've got them in silver, red, black, and bi-coloured. Reports coming in all the time. In case you still want to go, I ought to tell you that three of the 5th Minesweeping Flotilla working from Harwich have just been bombed by Jerry planes. And you won't find any of ours up there." Not so welcoming now, mused Ouvry.

This was really the last straw. He sent his appraisal of the situation to Flag Officer, Humber. "You are not to proceed until air cover is provided," came back the answer, and the operation was over before it had begun.

"I don't know how you feel about it, Chief," said Ouvry, "but I'm sure we'd never have caught a mine out there—let alone get it ashore. We'll be able to take our pick of these along the Yorkshire coast any day now, anyway, for surely they'll be driven ashore by this ghastly south-easter?"

Hardly had he stopped speaking when the phone rang in the office of the Naval Control Service, the Grimsby home they had found for themselves. "Is Lieutenant-Commander Ouvry there? I've got a mine for him." The rating passed the receiver over. "Oh, Ouvry, it's F.O., Humber, here. There's a mine ashore near Bridlington—black, with horns; probably British. Thought I'd better let you know, as you're in the vicinity."

As the reports of mines had been received, remembering the German broadcast of a defensive field off Heligoland, Ouvry had realized that all these specimens must have broken free of their sinkers in the storm and sailed in armada style across the North Sea, driven before the south-easter.

The latest report of a horned mine ashore confirmed this.

"Excuse me, sir," he said, "but I don't think you'll find it is British. I'm pretty sure it's one of a German field from over the other side. The nearest British field is down at Dover, and one couldn't have been washed up from there. I suggest it would be best if we came up to Bridlington and dealt with this one. It shouldn't be too hard. It's not the sample Admiralty are looking for, but we can't pick and choose."

"All right, Ouvry; you have my authority. Go ahead and get your mine, but be quick about it—and look after yourselves." The Admiral rang off.

So they had made contact at last. This looked reasonably straightforward. All being well, a horn mine was comparatively routine stuff—as far as anything could be said to be.

Just before dawn on Thursday, October 12, Ouvry and Baldwin, with A.B.'s Vearncombe and Farrand, chartered a taxi in Grimsby. "Take us to Hull as quickly as you can, will you?" Ouvry asked, telling Baldwin that he had arranged for a naval car to meet them there for the second stage of the journey. After six weeks of frustration Ouvry was glad to be off. Along the banks of the Humber they ran into murky morning fog, which slowed them down to a maddening crawl. At last they reached New Holland for the ferry over to Hull—only to find it was not running because of the gloom.

Ouvry went over to the ferryman. "Can't you possibly get us across, please?"

"Sorry, sir; till I can see barrage balloon I can't take 'ee t'other side." He was adamant. The first ferry of the day must wait. Two hours dragged by. Finally the fog cleared and they were across. A second car, in what was to be the all-too-familiar khaki colour, with R.N. inscribed on the windscreen, whisked them on to Bridlington—and beyond, to Sewerby. The fog had gone now, and Flamborough Head loomed out of an autumn morning as the four of them contacted the local coastguard.

"There's your mine." The Yorkshireman pointed down two hundred and fifty feet of cliff to a dark speck on the shore between high- and low-water marks. It looked far-off, unreal, but as they worked their way along the base of the cliff, scrambling over the rocks, it gradually assumed shape and substance. Ouvry was quite relieved to be face to face with it at last. This was what they had all been waiting for, even though it wasn't the answer to Aldeburgh. Meanwhile it was something to be going on with—a job in hand.

The tide was on the flood, borne strongly in by the south-easter, still unabated. Time was short. Running over the last rocks, they suddenly saw it. German without a doubt. It had horns; the black outer paint had partially worn off, leaving a red undercoat exposed. Its mechanism plate was buried in sand and rock. They dug a hole in the sand round the plate, and rolled the mine carefully clear, so that Ouvry could get to the detonator and primer.

"Careful a horn doesn't touch the deck," he warned. The detonator was withdrawn, slowly, surely. The wash of the water suddenly sounded in Ouvry's ears. Before he had not been aware of it. Now, as he relaxed with the job half done, one of two fangs drawn, he heard the soft splashing—though it had been there lapping near them all the time. "Give me the spanner, Chief." He put it to the mechanism plate, adjusted it to fit the German nuts securing the plate, then one by one undid them, taking out the primer. The horns were harmless, so two were taken off, together with other oddments. They could not get the mine itself away.

"Tide's coming in, sir," called out a local youth who was watching the operation, transfixed, from as near as he was allowed. "You won't get away at all unless you're quick. You'll have to swim for it—or shin up the cliff!" the lad added, with the cheerful air of the young when disclosing momentous intelligence. But the quartet did not mind now. The worst was over. But just before they were ready to quit, in their hurry they got some of the explosive on their hands. No proper chemicals were available.

"Come on," said Ouvry; "hurry up. We'll have to wash them in the sea; the salt should do the trick. But be quick about it. If you don't develop dermatitis you'll drown!" Back at Sewerby, Ouvry went to see the local constable, got a message through to the Admiralty and F.O., Humber, and realized that he was starving. None of them had eaten since before dawn at Grimsby. Now the afternoon was already waning.

"There's no restaurant hereabouts," confided the policeman, "and it's out of hours at the pub, but perhaps if we go along together we can persuade them to rattle up something."

The publican had just finished clearing up after the midday regulars when he was more than mildly astonished to hear a bang on the door and see the unmistakable helmet of the law silhouetted through the clouded-glass door. But he was even more alarmed to hear a request he never thought to reach his ears from the village bobby: "These four gentlemen want some beer and cheese, Alf. Serve them with it, will you, and there'll be no inquest afterwards!"

Alf, like all the village, had heard of the mine and the men who were down on the beach, so was glad to oblige, if a little dazed. The War had certainly been brought home to him that day. And if he had flouted the licensing laws, with the connivance of authority, he had the consolation that Ouvry too was breaking one of the strictest naval codes—by drinking his mild-and-bitter with the other three!

Back at *Vernon*, Ouvry ran into his newly arrived First Lieutenant along the passage outside M's room. The Lieutenant ("Number One") was the first real reinforcement that his little "rendering-safe" party had had.

"Glad to see you back safe and sound, sir," Number One said. "I'm sorry your Sewerby mine wasn't the first, but I couldn't really refuse to go up to Wrabness, could I, sir? And it would happen a few days before yours, wouldn't it?" His eyes were twinkling wickedly.

Ouvry took out a little exercise-book, ruled red lines down it, and wrote on the cover: "German Fireworks." Inside he recorded: "Type X; date, 6/10/39; place, Wrabness; rendered safe by Number One." Under this: "Type Y; date 12/10/39; place, Bridlington; rendered safe by Lt-Cdr Ouvry."

After this German horn mines began to come ashore by the dozen all along the East Coast, so that in the next weeks about two hundred were successfully handled without loss. C.P.O. Baldwin operated between Spurn Head and Scarborough, and Lieutenant Anderson and Number One both found full employment.

After the first spate of X and Y types Lieutenant-Commander Roy Edwards came across the first Z type. He had been made Rendering Mines Safe Officer, Nore Command, and accepted the challenge of such an appointment in the spirit of the swashbuckler. He set up base at Great Yarmouth, where he and his three ratings

(C.P.O. Spriggs and A.B.'s Keen and Wilson) were enjoying a twenty-four hours' break before flitting to North Norfolk to continue operations. But at 0830 on the morning of the 3rd a signal from the coastguard at Garton sent them scurrying to Bakers Score, where they found a mine much smaller than those discovered to date, half buried in the beach.

Removing the sand from around the base, they saw one, two, then three, long steel spikes projecting, together with five ordinary horns on top. Gradually the mechanism plate was exposed, a mirror held underneath, and the plate seen to be like that of the Y type handled by Ouvry, but smaller. The switch on the outside was set to E, which they first took to mean that it should have exploded on breaking adrift. Edwards changed his mind about it later, though, concluding that it was meant to explode the mine on hitting a beach. But the soft sand had protected the horns, and the switch had not fired. At closer quarters he decided that the spikes were horns too. Holes dug around the shell allowed the horns to clear as it was tilted and rolled over to expose the mechanism plate. Having done this, the four of them withdrew to discuss the next step.

"The orders from Admiralty and *Vernon* are that mines with switches set to E are to be exploded from a safe distance, and not rendered," Edwards told them. "But as this is obviously new—even though it's not magnetic or acoustic—I think it's up to us to tackle it."

"Aye, aye, sir; I'm with you," said Spriggs quickly.

"As it happens, that's just what I'm planning, Chief, so I'm glad you've volunteered!" A chuckle ran round the four of them, which relieved feelings a little. Edwards went on: "Keen and Wilson, there's no point in all of us being in on this just for the sake of it, so I'll have to tell you two to wait over here while the Chief and I get on with it."

Not without some qualms, Edwards and Spriggs got the detonator out, found it had fired, and so should have fired the mine, and then went over to see why the primer had not dropped. Its end was badly pitted. They were safe.

So much for their twenty-four hours off duty.

Two and a half years later, within sight of this very spot, Edwards and an American ensign were to meet disaster.

All the while these interludes were in progress the original mine menace grew—off the Thames and Portland, in the Firth of Forth, and in the Bristol Channel. On November 13 the cruiser-minelayer *Adventure* was severely damaged by a mine off the Tongue light-vessel in the Thames Estuary. The destroyer *Blanche*, in her company, fared worse and was sunk. German destroyers probably laid this field the previous night, and it was seriously successful. At least six ships succumbed in a straight line. *Mastiff* was mined, and sank working with one of the *Vernon* Mine Recovery Flotilla, trying to trawl up specimens of Hitler's secret weapon. Between the 18th and 22nd fifteen merchant-ships suffered the fate of being mined too, including the passenger ships *Simon Bolivar* and *Terukini Maru*—Dutch and Japanese respectively. In the chill of the Firth of Forth the cruiser *Belfast* actuated another mine, to be put out of action for over a year. Clearly the situation had become critical. Neutrals were endangered as much as our own ships.

The blood of Britain's lifeline flowed free, heart-rendingly so. The country carried on, blissfully ignorant of the full force of the drama being played out in the wings, as it were. The arteries of her sea-lanes could not be cut for long if the country were to survive. Then, on the night of November 21, the Luftwaffe laid parachute mines in the Thames, Humber, and Stour-Orwell estuaries. All incoming and outgoing traffic stopped: the arteries froze. The situation deteriorated from grey to grim. The destroyer *Gipsy* was sunk in the Channel off Harwich. Anti-aircraft opposition to the planes was scanty, so was augmented by Lewis guns posted on the end of Southend Pier. And what anti-aircraft batteries the Army had in Essex were not allowed to open fire on aircraft without first obtaining permission from Uxbridge! Naval gunners could fire—and did—as they were not part of our authorized defences! Pitiful, perhaps, but to those aware of the true position—desperate.

2

Magnetic Mine

PALE, pellucid moonlight streamed over the sleeping city on the night of November 21–22, streaking the harbour with quicksilver shafts. Over in the dockyard a crane creaked as it swung something ashore—a bundle for Britain, outlined in the night. Smoke rose from the power-station. Otherwise all was still.

Suddenly in the office of the Duty Mining Officer at H.M.S. *Vernon* the phone rang. The time: 0215. The caller: the Captain of *Vernon*.

"It's the Captain speaking. I've just had a call from Admiralty, and I want to get hold of Commander M. If he's not there please give me his number at home."

"I'm sorry, sir; he's not on duty to-night. But I've got his home number, if you'll wait just a second. He lives at Alverstoke, but the exchange is Gosport 61."

"Thanks. I'll ring him there."

Captain D. W. Boyd flashed the *Vernon* operator with an impatient forefinger and asked for the number.

"Sayer? It's Captain Boyd this end. Sorry to drag you out of your bunk at this Godforsaken hour, but Admiralty have been through. There's a change in the mine situation, it seems—and one for the worse. The Thames, Humber, and Stour-Orwell are bunged up with them. D.M.S. wants you to send some one up to

Whitehall first thing in the morning. Sooner or later they hope we'll be able to get hold of one."

The drill to meet this contingency had already been well rehearsed.

"I'll get straight on to Ouvry, sir, and get him on the move."

Sayer was strangely still for a moment before calling the Titchfield number. They had discussed the drill that must be carried out when faced with such a situation. Everything had been building up to it. But now it was nearly here, only a matter of days, probably, the full implication of it all surged back to him.

Unhurried, he said, "Titchfield 2361, please, operator." He looked at his watch, then round the room of his flat in Alverstoke. Minutes passed. It was 0225.

The operator was on the line. "Sorry, caller, but I can't get the ringing tone. It seems to be unobtainable."

This would happen, Sayer mused. Eleven weeks of war we've been waiting, and this is the time the phone picks to go wrong. He asked the operator to try again, but there was no response. "Could you give me the Fareham police station, then, please?" he asked. A pause, then a sleepy "Hello."

"Is that the police? I'm sorry to disturb you, but this is Commander Sayer, of H.M.S. *Vernon*, Portsmouth. I'm speaking from my home at Alverstoke. I've been trying to get through to a Lieutenant-Commander Ouvry on a Titchfield number, but the line's out of order. I've got urgent naval orders for him, so I'd be grateful if you can get some one along to his house. The address is Somerfields, Peak Lane."

"Ah, yes, I know it, sir; live along towards Titchfield myself. And what shall we tell him?"

"Just ask him to ring Commander Sayer at Gosport 61, will you?"

Sayer got back on to the Duty Mining Officer at *Vernon*.

"Oh, Sub, it's Commander M. Lieutenant-Commander Ouvry is wanted urgently at Admiralty in the morning, and I can't get through on the phone. I've asked a bobby to go round to his house, but just in case he doesn't find it, nip round to Fareham, will you, and ask him to phone me?"

It was 0303. Somerfields was swathed in sleep. But a moment later the limb of the law thundered on the front door. At first no response was forthcoming. The constable's torch met the reflecting brass of a ship's bell hanging overhead on the porch. It crossed his mind to sound it. The rope hung temptingly. But one more thump, and the household was awake. Ouvry groped his way downstairs.

Lorna heard the maddening murmur of half-heard voices; then the door closed. "Is anything wrong, John?" she called.

"I've got to ring Sayer. He couldn't get a line apparently. I hope outgoing calls are all right."

"Ah, Ouvry, glad you've got through. It's a hell of an hour to worry you, but things are moving faster, it seems." Sayer recounted the latest news. "D.M.S. want you up there on the first train. I don't know what you can do until something more concrete turns up, but you'd better be on tap. The odds are that if one is found it will be pretty near London, so you'll save time by being up there. I don't like giving you this order, Ouvry. But don't worry about things back here. I'll keep your wife in touch and let her know exactly how things are going."

"Thanks, sir. I suppose it's no picnic, but I don't mind much now."

"Take care, then."

The bedroom was cosy, with leaded windows and an unmistakably English look about it.

"I have to go up to Town first thing, darling. They've dropped some more from aircraft, and there's just a chance of one turning up somewhere. I may be away for a few days. I don't know any more than that at the moment."

Lorna had known this was bound to come sooner or later. Three A.M. could hardly have been a worse time. There was an unreality about the whole world just then. A quiet night . . . the Maginot Line . . . England sleeping . . . Robin and Philip too . . . John's high cheeks, grey-flecked hair . . . blue eyes looking into hers . . . the double black-out curtains. Before dawn filtered through them she was up getting breakfast, and in a matter of minutes, it seemed, he was ready. "God bless you, John," she whispered. At the door he kissed her—and was gone. First light flushed in the ship's bell. Lorna went indoors to see to the boys.

The Service car got him over to Portsmouth Harbour station in good time for the first fast to Waterloo. John glanced instinctively over to the right as it drew slowly away from the platform, in time to see the scurry of sailors going 'aboard' *Vernon.* Another ordinary day. He was genuinely glad now that something else presented itself—even if it had yet to take shape. Fading were the painted figureheads of old ships adorning the roadway into *Vernon*. Below the high embankment the United Services rugger ground, where he had played so often before the War. The tall mining-tank vanished behind the Guildhall. Past Havant, the train gained speed again. As he looked out, left this time, he saw two country-houses standing serene amid the bare branches of November. West Leigh House and West Leigh Cottage. Hither the following autumn were to come Commander M's group and the civilian trials sections of Mine Design Department when Portsmouth became too hot a place for handling mines. The terrace of West Leigh House overlooked soft lawns that spoke of another century far from 1939.

Through Godalming, Farncombe, to the river Wey, winding placidly round St Catherine's. Just before the tunnel into the hill and Guildford, Ouvry saw the clear, clean grass slopes of Pewley Down, and in the distance the tiny church atop St Martha's Hill. The Pilgrim's Way. Their mission one of peace. How different his! Or was it, really? Perhaps he was a pilgrim. Perhaps they would have understood. They must have strained sinews to cross the hills and dales. Canterbury their goal. His destination—unknown. But he felt an affinity to them across the centuries.

At the Director of Mine-sweeping (D.M.S.) division Ouvry asked for Captain Morse. He was shown into a Georgian-looking office, and saw a strained face. "Good to see you, Ouvry. Sorry I'm not at my best, but it's been a pretty gruelling night. Reports are coming in all the time. If it's not mines dropping it's ships going down. You may like to be working something out. It seems generally agreed from signals received that the

mines look like sailors' kitbags suspended from parachutes. If only they were as harmless! As for the losses,

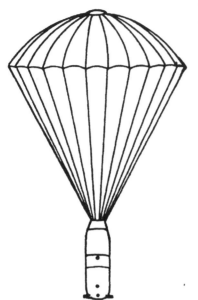

the latest is the *Gipsy*.
Naturally we suspect mag-
netics are responsible for the
new batch of sinkings this
week, but there's still no
proof—and nothing conclu-
sive we can do in the way
of antidotes till we get the
proof. I've sent people down
to Southend, Harwich, and
Grimsby to get all the details they can, to talk to the
men who've been wrecked.
We'll have to wait for their
reports."

Ouvry was given a desk in one of the outer offices,
and found the ordinarily august organization of the
Admiralty in the grip of a mounting sense of frustration, which conveyed itself to him in some measure as
he sat trying to clear his mind and get his ideas down on
paper about the possible appearance of the mine, and
the way it worked. He concluded that it might be
magnetic or acoustic, and a ground mine. But as it was
liable to fire when removed to shallow water—less than
fifteen feet, say—the only evident way of dealing with
it would be for a diver to unfit and unprime it under
water; after which the weapon could be hoisted to the
surface. Alternatively, to bore holes in the vicinity of
its firing source and flood it. Again, the mine could be
retrieved in safety. This was all to some extent conjec-
tural, however, as circumstances would have to be

treated on their merits entirely, and theory was liable to complete revision in the cold light of fact.

The day dragged by. Later on Morse sent for Ouvry again.

"We've had further signals from Hull and Grimsby, but they're not much help, I'm afraid, Ouvry. The skipper of the *Yarmouth Trader*, for instance: he's said they sighted a large bundle attached to a 'chute descending fast into seven fathoms. Anderson is up there now. The *Yarmouth Trader* marked the position of the object by a dan in mid-channel. Admiralty permission was then given to offer a thousand pounds to a diver to go down and investigate, but in view of subsequent developments the same day and night at Southend this became unnecessary."

At that point a Wren entered the room. "Excuse me, sir; Lieutenant-Commander Lewis has just got back to Admiralty and would like to see you."

"Good. Show him in, will you? I was just going to tell you about him, Ouvry. He's been down to Southend all day trying to find out the facts—and if we can get to any of last night's batch. Ah, Lewis, Ouvry has come up from *Vernon*, and I suggest you two have a chat to settle a plan of campaign in case anything turns up."

"Certainly, sir. We'll leave you for the time being, and report back later if we don't hear from you in the meanwhile."

Ouvry and Lewis made their way through the labyrinth of corridors that is the Admiralty, and eventually found the canteen and a hot meal. Over a rationed rissole Lewis explained how he (under Rear-Admiral Lyster) had been switched to the investigation of mines only a few days earlier.

c

"Cameron, a Wavy Navy two-ringer, and I got out a nine-point programme, including visits to ships damaged and interviews with survivors. When the *Belfast* was mined on Tuesday Cameron left for Rosyth, and as the latest reports of laying began to come in I motored down to Southend at 0300 this morning. Armitage has gone to the Humber, as Morse may have told you, and Captain Barrett's at Harwich. You've most likely heard from them during the day."

Ouvry told him about the Grimsby episodes.

Lewis went on: " I've managed to fix the approximate position of three or four of the mines from observers, and I've got some information about the Hun's laying methods. I spent most of the day, in fact, talking to masters of merchant-ships lying off Southend who saw the thing dropping last night. It's all too easy for Adolf, Ouvry; there's hardly any effective ack-ack. But we'll do our damnedest to beat 'em somehow."

This man Lewis was certainly a tonic. Ouvry liked him immensely—his cheerfulness, everything about the robust, ruddy, and reliable colleague. But no one could offset the shadow which was cast across the old cobbled forecourt of the Admiralty that night as they strolled back to Morse's office.

"Go off and get some rest, Ouvry," the Captain advised. Both men were aware of the sense of strain; both had had a broken night. Morse wanted to be sure that Ouvry kept fresh in case he was wanted—fresh not only in body, but in mind, for he had to be alert. Lewis too left the Admiralty about the same time.

As Ouvry picked his way up to Trafalgar Square and turned sharp right into Northumberland Avenue Lorna switched off the bedroom light at Somerfields and settled into a restless kind of sleep. And at the same moment, too, a German seaplane was steering an unsteady course over the Thames Estuary—it was a moonless night—the pilot peering into the pitch void and driving rain, looking for bearings. Dimly he made out the river-mouth and prepared to run in on course. He came a little lower to be sure. Two hundred feet. One hundred and fifty feet. At that second the machine-gun outpost on the end of Southend Pier which Roger Lewis had organized only hours earlier shattered the night with a staccato series of bursts. Already in a state of nervous tension with the stress of night flying in filthy conditions, the pilot was shaken out of his wits by the guns. He was lower than he thought. He would never get away. Instinctively he pressed the button on his control panel, and his lethal load was released. Two bundles dropped through the night air for a few seconds, and almost before their parachutes had time to open Hitler's secret weapon number one was neatly deposited into the sea off Shoeburyness.

Local observers realized that the unknown objects might well be mines, and that they would most likely be uncovered at low water—0400. They had been dropped at high tide. A call was put through to the Admiralty as soon as it seemed sure that mines were the answer. D.M.S. phoned Ouvry. "Pack your bag and come straight over to Admiralty. It's Morse here, and we've got a Jerry mine for you." Ouvry had just dropped off into a first deep sleep at his hotel. For a second the words were meaningless. Then the whole wonder of them rushed round his brain. At last, thank God! The waiting's over! It's up to us!

Over in the D.M.S. office Lewis met him, and wasted

no words: "A 'chute mine's been sighted near Southend. I'm organizing transport, and have been in touch with the Navy down there. We've got to get down right away. It'll be dry in two or three hours. The car's coming at 0100. We've just time to peep in and see Admiral Lyster."

"Where is it exactly, Lewis?" the Admiral asked.

"On the mud-flats, more or less, at Shoeburyness, sir. We'll have to hurry—we don't know how long it will be dry for. The tide comes in miles round that coast in a matter of minutes, it seems, so we ought to be there just before low water."

"Right, you two; don't let me keep you. You've got my blessing. Take care of yourself, Ouvry. Leave all the organization to Lewis, and you just concentrate on the mine. That's an overtime job, anyway. I don't have to tell you, I know, but the orders are: recover it at all costs."

A knock at the door. A duty rating ventured in. "Car waiting at the front entrance, sir, for Southend."

"Now, look, Ouvry, you've got the key job, so you go in the back and try and get some sleep. It's not the sort of thing you can tackle if you're tired."

"But I'm perfectly all right," protested Ouvry.

"You're going to sleep—if I have to put you off myself! And, driver, we want you to make Southend as fast as humanly possible without wrecking the whole machine. I know the way, so I'll sit in front with you."

The driver took him at his word and crashed fifteen red lights before getting clear of the London area. They were approaching Shoeburyness faster than the tide was quitting it. The blacked-out traffic signals, with their

thin-slit crosses of light barely visible in the rain, became less and less frequent, until nothing could be seen
at all. The flat Essex road came at them with dull
regularity.

"It's no damned day-trip to Southend, this, is it?"
observed Lewis to the driver quietly, whose only response
was to grunt and dig his heel into the rubber flooring of
the car and press his toe forward on the accelerator.

0300: the Palace Hotel, Southend. Ghostlike. As in
some Priestley play—free of space and time. Fog had
come down during the last part of the journey and
slowed up what had looked like standing as a record run
to the holiday resort. As the car drew into the curved
drive Lewis turned back to Ouvry. "How did you sleep,
old man?"

"'Fraid I didn't. I remembered that I've left my
'rendering mines safe' notes on the dressing-table at the
hotel, so I've had to go through them all again in my
mind!"

"Well, I'll be damned!" Lewis exploded.

They parked their baggage, changed cars, picked up
Commander Bowles of N.O.I.C.'s staff, together with a
local photographer Bowles had managed to round up,
and proceeded along to Shoeburyness. As the car sped
past the Kursaal—dark silhouettes of a scenic railway—
Bowles told the others that one of the vessels held up out
in the tideway, a frozen-meat ship, had swung on the
turn of the tide about the time the new batch of mines
had been dropped, and just by this gentle action had fired
one of them. Whatever device it was firing the mines,
taking one to pieces was going to be no ordinary ordeal.

"By the way," went on Bowles, "although your job's
hard, there's one bit of luck. Shoeburyness is a military

station with an artillery range. They fire their missiles out over the mud and recover them at low water. So all the gear you want will be at hand; and there's a fully equipped workshop, too, you may be glad of before you've finished."

Ouvry thanked him for these encouragements. The sense of expectancy heightened.

At Shoeburyness Commander Maton met them with a party of soldiers. Bowles made the introductions. Ouvry told them: "I doubt if we'll be able to tackle it on this tide. Light is vital—and this rain makes it pretty well out of the question. We'll have to secure it and wait for the next low tide in the afternoon. Incidentally, I suppose you've located it all right? If so, let's get over and see it, shall we?"

"Everything's arranged for you," said Maton. "We've certainly found one, and we've got ropes and stakes, and here are some thigh-boots for you. Hope you can find the right size from this selection."

"Wait a second, though," Ouvry answered. "Before we go we'd better unload all the metal we're carrying. Money. Cigarette-cases. Everything. And what about buttons? They'll have to go, too; we can't chance anything."

So these came off, and the party moved forward.

It was 0400. A vile night. Black—and wet. A private led them, splashing through pools left by the ebbing tide. An Aldis lamp held aloft swayed to and fro crazily with each step, lighting small patches of the rippled sand. The private waded on. He it was who had seen the parachute dropping from Shoeburyness. Another few minutes passed; then he called out excitedly, "There it is ahead, sir."

To the rest of the party it was still out of range. They rushed up. "Don't go any nearer," warned Ouvry. He scanned the few remaining yards to where the soldier was pointing. His heart pounded. Ouvry and Lewis, torches in hand, moved towards it for a better look.

Here it was . . . the unknown quantity . . . inanimate object . . . one touch might animate it . . . blow them to bits. What was it? Magnetic? Acoustic? Cosmic? Could be any or all.

Out of the dark it seemed to edge towards them with each successive step they took. A black, glistening hippopotamus, sinister, shiny, looming into the torch-light. Half embedded in sand five hundred yards below high-water mark. A little pool encircling the end in the mud. Half a mile out to sea in the before-dawn chill of a November night. Excitement intensified on the rain-swept shore.

The winning of the War might depend on these next few hours.

More than the length of a man, it was. Nearly seven feet. And about two feet in diameter. Cylindrical, made of some aluminium alloy. That much they saw at once. Tubular horns on the rounded, embedded nose attracted their attention. Ouvry moved to the other end. Neither he nor Lewis spoke. An acoustic vibrator could respond to a voice—and anything might be inside. Ouvry pointed the tail out to Lewis. It was hollow and open, with a massive phosphor-bronze spring sticking out. Apparently this was where the parachute had been attached. Now no sign of it could be found. But the mine was the vital thing, and specifically two devilish devices near the nose, forward. Prominent on top of the mine, one was brass, one aluminium. The brass fitting Ouvry took to be a hydrostatic valve, which duly encouraged him. But the second was different from anything he had been used to, or seen on our own non-contact mines. The aluminium was polished, and secured by a screwed ring sealed with tallow. Another encouragement: attached was what seemed to be a "tear-off" strip, twisted but secure—possibly a safety arrangement.

Somehow, later that day, Ouvry had to find a way into the mine. These two fittings were the only visible means. Once off, it would be up to him to make the thing safe so that the secrets could be unlocked. But he was looking too far ahead. Now the first job was to consider what tools he would need. The mysterious second fitting seemed as if it would harbour the primer and detonator, so this would have to be tackled first. But no tools he had ashore came near to matching the ring securing the fitting. Nor would any of the non-magnetic tools which were coming up from *Vernon* in the morning do the job. A four-pin spanner was wanted, so Ouvry motioned to Lewis to take an impression of the aluminium fitting on a sheet of an Admiralty signal-pad. He placed the paper gently against the fitting, still more softly pressing it to the shape. Lewis handed the sheet to Ouvry, who passed it on to Maton.

Ouvry beckoned the photographers—one official, one the local commercial cameraman collected earlier. From every angle they took a series of flashlight pictures, the surrounding sand leaping into stippled relief, then becoming once more shrouded. Soldiers passed hemp-lines round the mine, and lashed them to the stakes plunged into the soft mud-sand. Ouvry and Lewis jotted down their final notes before stepping back—into the known again.

"Good work, chaps," Maton volunteered to all and sundry. Then to Ouvry: "You'll want a non-magnetic spanner made to unscrew the ring? I'll get the workshop to fix one in brass by noon. That should be in plenty of time for the tide. Some brass rods of all sizes might come in useful, too."

"That'll be fine. You're making it all as easy as it could be."

Making their way back to the beach, they came across the parachute, sodden with sand and sea. It seemed to weigh a ton, but a few good heaves brought it high and dry out of the reach of the tide.

"I should try and get a bit of rest if I were you," Maton told the two Lieutenant-Commanders. "I tell you what. Come along to my house—Bowles, you as well —and Ouvry and Lewis can have an hour at least before breakfast." Both of them felt too strong a sense of suppressed excitement to do more than doze, and at 0600 the dawn heralded a breakfast of fried eggs as a special treat. Ouvry felt better. He looked out over Southend to the incoming tide. As the two men made out their preliminary report and attached it to the photos of the mine which had just been printed they realized the responsibility resting on them. It seemed to outweigh the danger—although they were conscious of that too.

The phone rang. Maton took it. "Another one, you say? Three hundred yards away from the first? We'll be down at once." Then, turning to his guests: "No rest for the wicked. They've sighted a second mine near the first."

In a matter of minutes they were at the nearest point to the stretch of beach. Drawing on their waders for the second time in a few hours, they lunged into the deepening water to try to locate it. But the tide was flooding fast. An old man looked out of a still-older hulk moored near by. "You won't find it now," he called over to them. "It's been covered for some minutes. But it'll be dry again at low water." They decided to wait for the falling tide for this one, as for the other.

Ouvry took a call from Sayer at *Vernon* during the morning. "We'll be able to tackle it early P.M.," Ouvry told him, "and will let you know the result as soon as we can. There's only one other thing on my mind. Lewis and I are busy preparing the plan of attack, so I wonder if you'd mind giving my wife a ring for me. I'd be very grateful."

"My dear Ouvry, I was going to do so, anyway, the second I had put down the receiver. And it's we who should be grateful—not you. Best of luck again."

Soon afterwards Baldwin and Vearncombe arrived with the rest of the tools, direct from *Vernon*. It was good to see them, Ouvry thought. The Chief, completely and utterly loyal, the epitome of all that was best among non-commissioned officers. No more than medium height, with a weathered face. And young Vearncombe, the tall, good-looking two-badge A.B.—as reliable as the Chief. Yes, it was certainly good to have these two with him. And Lewis, a tower of strength and support. Lewis, responsible for the organization, Ouvry for the technical job of tackling the mine.

"Now that we've settled the best method of attack," Ouvry suggested to Lewis, "I think the only sensible procedure is to split the four of us into groups in case of accidents. That will double our chances, and the second pair may be able to profit from any miscalculations.

There's the other mine left for them. That's the deciding factor as I see it."

"If it's really the way you want it," yielded Lewis grudgingly.

"Baldwin and I have got the background for this sort of thing—as far as anyone has—so we'll kick off, and you and Vearncombe can wait on the foreshore. I'll signal each move I make, and you can tick them off the list, so you'll know how far I've got. I'll wave both hands above my head after each episode. But don't feel left out in the cold, for I've a hunch that we'll all be needed before the day's out—one way or the other."

There was no hint of drama in his voice. He was just stating facts.

It was 1300. Neither of them felt like lunch. The tide had fallen clear of both mines. Maton and some of the soldiers took up a sheltered position on the foreshore opposite the mines. A tractor lorry with a crane attached stood by hopefully, for the time when one of them would be ready for collection. While the military photographer took a series of daylight pictures, with long rulers to mark the length and height of the thing, Ouvry and Lewis strolled over to look at the second specimen. Like number one, its nose was nuzzled down deep into the sand, but the whole thing was on a different slew, leaving a large plate exposed which could not be seen on the first. The horns, they concluded, were in no way dangerous, merely projections to bury in the sea-bed and keep the mine steady, so that it would not roll with the pressure of the water. That was one item less to worry about—but plenty remained. Night had passed, but all was still mystery. A live acoustic mine might kill at the first touch on its shell. A magnetic mine might equally easily explode. Both were liable to have some German device to stop their secrets being shared—a booby-trap that might go off as the first nut was loosened.

The time had reached 1330. Ouvry thought of his wife as he and Baldwin waved to Lewis and Vearncombe.

Sayer had told her of the plan. He did not tell her not to worry. At 1330 she cleared away the boys' dishes and knew the operation was on. Pounding from the radio, the wild waves of a Sibelius symphony broke over her emotions. But in the midst of their turmoil she sensed a strange calm. She looked out over the Solent. A destroyer was ploughing over the Stokes Bay course, where British magnetic mines were being tested. The Isle of Wight car-ferry plodded slowly from the mainland. But few ships sailed otherwise. No channel was safe from the air, not even the Solent. John must manage it.

Lorna looked out again through the little leaded panes, as John had done only a matter of weeks before, when war was declared. The flowers had faded from the garden scene; the beds were bare. The lawn swept away round to the left in the arc John had meticulously measured a summer or so ago.

Beyond the low hedge at the bottom of the grass the branches of the fruit-trees wavered in the wind, bobbing bare in a November breeze. And over to the right of the little orchard—in the far corner of the garden, in fact—stood the "seven dwarfs' house." For visitors to Somerfields it was the showpiece. The family never showed it off, but people just fell in love with it automatically, and insisted on seeing all over it—adults especially.

To-day it stood serene, but silent. When it was built,

at the same time as the house two or three years earlier, Lorna had visions of a little girl playing in it. Then Philip was born. Both the boys liked the place, but it seemed to sense that it was made for a girl, and had not yet entirely fulfilled its purpose.

From the outside the little house looked a perfect replica of a country cottage. Built of real brick, standing ten feet tall, and with a gable facing the front. Lorna looked absent-mindedly at its turquoise window-frames, dainty rust shutters, and tiles the same as on Somerfields itself. The chimney-stack on the extreme right rose sheer, beyond the brick archway round the front door. No one was playing there to-day. As if the boys had become caught up in the War, too, and realized that the days moved momentously—for their country and their father.

Lorna remembered the night they had all spent in the little cottage; Robin had insisted that they sleep there on the first fine summer occasion of the year. And of the table-tennis in its one room, whose ceiling was the under-sides of the steeply sloping roof—the ball bouncing gaily in a pre-war world. . . .

Ouvry and Baldwin walked quickly over to the mine. A few paces off Ouvry saw a little brass ring reclining in the sand. "That looks as if it may be the missing part to that spindle of the top brass fitting, Chief. Yes, it is —look. I feel better already. Now let's forget the brass hat and concentrate on the aluminium one! You can see the shell's aluminium too. The black paint's chipped off still more after last night. Now, how about that fitting?"

1837. Baldwin handed him the four-pin spanner.

Ouvry looked closely into the fitting and saw a small plate, jointed with tallow, an oval-shaped groove filled with black wax, a screwed recess, and the copper "tear-off" strip he had seen in the early hours. The strip was masking one of the holes for the spanner. Baldwin went to pull it off. But Ouvry stopped him.

"Don't do that. It may be some safety device. Just turn it back carefully."

The Chief complied.

Ouvry tried the Shoeburyness-made spanner. "It fits," he whispered. His throat was parched. The wind had dried his lips too. A whining, wintry wind.

This was it. The moment had come at last. Moving the spanner unbelievably slowly, he unscrewed the ring a fraction of a turn. Nothing happened. They were still alive. Ten degrees . . . twenty . . . ninety . . . one-eighty . . . a whole turn. All was still well. He glanced up at the Chief. Another turn. A few more. And the ring was free.

"A rod, Chief."

Baldwin offered a choice. Ouvry took the smallest, jammed it into the opening. He took what he saw inside to be either a detonator or some sort of magnetic-needle device. Either was dynamite. Again at a crawl, holding the rod delicately, with precision, he lowered it into the opening, angler-like. The hook on the end looped over the fitting, and he withdrew his catch, a fraction of an inch at a time. It slid smoothly up. Ouvry was sweating now. Spray in the wind sprinkled his face. His waders stuck in the mud, then squelched free. If this were the detonator he had only to drop it once. There would be no second chance—not for him, anyway. Inch by inch it came. Then it was out. Back inshore,

Lewis adjusted his glasses more finely. "He's got something. Look, the Chief has signalled. Thank God for that much."

1349. Ouvry peered down into the dark void the fitting had left. Dimly he saw a pocket containing a tubular disc of explosive and a primer. And under the disc two more solid discs. He fished for these, this time with a brass rod filed to a pointed end. But they would not come free.

"Never mind, Chief. Let's look at what we've caught, and leave the one that's got away for the moment."

A cylindrical cup was screwed into the underside of the fitting in his hand, which was evidently the detonator —or, at least, *a* detonator.

"I think this is it, Chief. If it's the detonator the worst is over. But we'll have to take a look at the underneath of the mine. Run ashore and fetch the others to help manhandle it. We couldn't budge it an inch alone."

"Aye, aye, sir."

1404. Ouvry suddenly felt good. He breathed deeply. The strong Southend air reached the lining of his lungs. That *must* be the detonator. And if it is the firing source, what have we got to worry about? Nothing—much.

Looking away south, he saw the end of Southend Pier. No one stirred on it, save the naval gun-crew Lewis had organized. A good job I've got some one with some organization. The wind again, coming in short, blustering bursts over the mud-flats. The pools of water left by the tide quivered as it whipped at them. Over on the Southend cliffs he made out momentarily a royal-blue trolley-bus. So life was going on normally. Out here it was as if they were marooned. On an island of space and time. With a sea of mud enveloping them. The Chief had reached the others. The three of them were hurrying out now. Ouvry felt quietly confident. But at the back of his mind stuck obstinately the suggestion that the day's work was not yet over.

"It's too early to be too excited," he told Lewis, who was approaching him warmly, "but, all being well—all will be well. Can you help turn it? We might just manage it between us."

With ropes they nearly did it. As they paused, thinking they would have to enlist the aid of the Army after all, a lone figure, complete with bull-terrier, threaded his way out to them.

"Hello, there!" called Ouvry. "It's Dr Wood, isn't it?"

"That's right. I was up at Admiralty when your message came through this morning, so I hurried down to see how it's going."

"Right in the thick of it now. Just at this second you've come quite providentially to bend a fifth pair of shoulders—or lend a fifth pair of hands. We've got to turn it as quickly as we can. The tide will be coming in again in an hour or two."

1422. Dr Wood, chief scientist of the Mine Design Department at *Vernon*, just tilted the scales. The underside rolled clear, coated with damp mud-sand. It was now about 120 degrees round from its former position, so that both top and bottom fittings were accessible. Ouvry could collect the loose primer discs he had not been able to reach at the earlier angle. Just as on mine number two, this one had a plate flush with the shell, diametrically opposed to the brass "hydrostatic valve" on top. This was confidently unscrewed. Beneath it appeared a circular screwed bung with four recesses. No spanner seemed suitable to shift it, so some elementary force had to be applied. This took time.

1457. There seemed to be no end to the gadgets— like forcing a way through an eternal jungle, with each bush thicker than the last. So it wasn't going to be as easy as Ouvry had thought.

Another screwed plate met the gaze of the little company. Two terminals mounted neatly on it had two leads winding away out of sight through a hole into the bowels. No-man's-land. Suddenly it occurred to him that *this was the main detonator circuit*—and not the other. It all had to be gone through again, but an air of confidence pervaded the scene now. Still in slow motion, Ouvry twisted both leads round and round in turn till each strand of each wire snapped under the strain. Then he insulated them. Break an electrical circuit— always a good policy. No spanner fitted the screws securing the plate, so a non-magnetic screwdriver filled the bill.

As he took the plate out Ouvry saw that it was a detonator carrier with an electric detonator similar to that used on the German horned mines. Out it came— and he felt on top of the world.

1510. He could not see to get at the primer from this side, so the mine was rolled back, the original brass fitting taking up its position on top. This was the continuation of the detonator-primer pocket. Ouvry undid the cover with a spanner, and, as if to echo their elation, the fitting inside leaped out under the force of a strong spring! After a general surge back—and a chorus of relief—the long phosphor-bronze spring followed it, cascading high into the air, before coming to rest in the

D

wash of the incoming tide. The priming charge was easily removed, and there remained only a large hydrostatic arming-clock.

1527. Triumphant, all four of them signalled gaily to the soldiers inshore for the tractor and crane. The five leads to the clock were cut, and the trophies carted ashore.

By 1600 it was all over. The mine was hoisted into the lorry, and sent away for safe storage overnight under cover. The light was failing, so no attempt was made to get to the second mine, in any case already awash.

Up on the beach they all stretched out in glorious relaxation. Lewis laid the arming-clock down. Straightway it started ticking. All four of them hurtled away from it! They were all too well aware of the chance of booby-traps to risk anything at this stage.

"Nothing to worry about," laughed Ouvry. "It's only the spindle." And all really was well at last.

At 1630 they took a combined lunch-tea. And by 1700 a report to the Admiralty informed their Lordships at the naval nerve-centre that Hitler's secret weapon number one was lying harmlessly in a Shoeburyness shed, awaiting transport to *Vernon* the following morning.

There remained the mysterious first aluminium fitting Ouvry had removed. He elected to stay overnight at Southend, so that he could take it on to Woolwich Arsenal, where Captain Barrett had arranged to have it inspected.

Lewis left for Whitehall, summoned to attend a Board of Admiralty at 2315 the same evening. A company of almost a hundred was waiting for him in the largest room of the Admiralty, and Lewis was overwhelmed to find himself seated between Winston Churchill and Admiral Sir Dudley Pound, with these distinguished men dwelling on his every word, only too conscious of all that had been at stake.

"Come on, now, Lewis; we want the whole story," Mr Churchill coaxed.

"Of course, sir. But I must stress that it was a combined operation, and I wish Lieutenant-Commander Ouvry and the others were here too."

Then he retraced the events of an eventful day—all twenty-four hours of it. Midnight came as he reached the end of the tale.

"Thank you, Lieutenant-Commander." The First Lord spoke for every one there—and millions more as yet unaware of the debt. "I'm going to get right through to *Vernon* now and tell them that we want to know what it is without delay, and that work must proceed day and night to this end. Only when we've got their verdict can we put counter-measures into effect, and every hour is beginning to count."

Ouvry met H. J. Taylor, of Mine Design Department, the following morning. Together they made their way to Woolwich with the aluminium fitting. What was the secret of this tiresome little thing? It was suspected of being some sort of time-fuse.

"We'd better try and open it up now, I suppose," suggested the Woolwich boffin. "If you'll pass it over, please, Ouvry."

Ouvry handed it to him. Between them it slithered to the floor! Although it contained explosive, they survived, for no report rent the air. Standing behind a metal ramp, having secured the fitting to clamps, the

scientist manipulated rods to take it apart. The detonator envelope was unscrewed and left at Woolwich for
analysis of its contents.

"Thanks for your help," said Ouvry as he left. "We'll
see what *Vernon* make of the rest of it." Stripped and
examined at Portsmouth, the fuse was found to be a
device for enabling the mine to be used as a delay-action
bomb—and used it was subsequently, all too familiarly,
as a land mine.

By tea-time on the 24th the mine reached *Vernon*.
Ouvry had phoned through first thing to say that it was
on its way. At about 1600, guarded by Baldwin and
Vearncombe, the monster rolled through the gate of
Vernon on the lorry—harmless now, but still an unknown
quantity scientifically. Mr Churchill's message had been
safely received, and was at once put into practice. The
post-mortem took place in the non-magnetic laboratory
building where operations went on behind locked doors,
and free from disturbance. Sentries guarded the door,
and a small team of civilian scientists picked from Mine
Design Department set to work—Dr Wood, Mr Kelly,
and Mr Shaw, together with Commander Sayer and
C.P.O. Baldwin.

A writer was detailed to keep an account of what was
done, and other experts co-opted at various stages.
Stripping and examination went on continuously throughout the night. Gradually, painstakingly—for science
cannot be rushed—the whole intricate mechanism began
to make sense. By 0200 on the 25th the verdict was pronounced—a magnetic mine. One-millionth part or less
of the current needed to light a torch was enough to fire
the mine, and this was generated by the magnetism of a

ship passing over it. By dawn their report was complete. From this knowledge steps immediately initiated soon resulted in the suggested solution—de-gaussing or de-magnetization of vessels.

Almost to the hour the tale was taken up again. As the little group of sleepy scientists filed quietly out of *Vernon* in the early light of Saturday morning, the 25th —midgets beneath the giant mining-tank, with its sixty feet or so of water for trials—Number One, who had been with them all night, gleaning what information he could about the mine, left with Baldwin and Vearncombe, bound for Shoeburyness and the second mine.

Number One could hardly wait to get to grips, even though he had grown attached to *Vernon* in the short time he had known the place. The wardroom block looked out to the jetty where H.M.S. *Plover* or *Vesuvius* was lying at anchor—he could never tell which was which. They were going out laying our mines. He and Ouvry and the rest were taking Jerry's to pieces. Futile sort of war! The pride-of-*Vernon* soccer pitch running alongside the little roadway was being marked out by an early-morning working-party for a match in the after-noon. Almost encroaching on the touchline, air-raid shelters were straddled. The flower-beds between the grass and the roadway looked a bit bare. Spring seemed years off. Never mind, he had enough to occupy him without fretting over flowers. One of the early ferries from Gosport jolted against the jetty up-harbour a little from the *Vernon* pier. Men hurried off, headed for the dockyard. Grey figures in a grey light. He was off in another direction. The car slid smoothly under the

Vernon archway, through the city, across the tram-lines —some still seemed to survive—and over the bridge at Hilsea. Off the island of Portsea.

It was 1600 before they came face to face with the second mine.

Their hastily made non-magnetic tools delighted in slipping. It was not without some fumbling that they succeeded in removing the cover-plate and its bung. The mine was awash with the tide as Number One got the detonator out. The wintry dusk came down. The next step was to roll the mine over so that the bomb-fuse was uppermost—but the nose stuck solid in the wet sand, and its hollow horns exercised a powerful suction-grip. Nine men working with hand-spikes could not shift it. Commander Maton came to the rescue, and a long rope was hitched on to an Army lorry, which moved into top gear. The slack snapped out of the rope. It quivered taut. And the monster rolled reluctantly over on to its other side, as if disturbed in heavy slumber. Deepening dusk and water underlined the likeness, transporting the scene into one of quiet nightmare.

With the water six inches deep, they started on the bomb-fuse. The spanner did not fit well. At last Number One got it to grip. The keep-ring was wrenched half a turn—and stopped. He swung it another revolution. A pistol-sharp 'click' cracked out from the depths of the dark inside. Number One glanced at Baldwin. An hour's tension snapped. Both men tore off the beach like scalded cats. A hundred yards clear, they paused. Wavelets washed inshore. The mine lay there subdued, still. Sitting in the water, just visible, looking at them evilly. Laughing to itself.

"Come on, Chief," the Lieutenant proposed. "What

we need is a hot bath and a good meal, and no more toying about to-night. It's too damned dark."

"I'm with you, sir. Thought we'd seen the last of
Vernon gates. . . ."

"And the first of the pearly gates, eh?" Number One
chuckled. "Never mind, Chief; we're still here."

At 0700, Sunday, November 26, the bomb-fuse surrendered gracefully, almost timidly, and the mine had
lost all its bravado of the previous night. Just a shell
now, with no venom left in it. Praise the Lord, thought
Number One.

"Why won't you tell me what it's all about, John?"

Lorna guessed it was something good from his sly
smile whenever she mentioned it.

"I've told you already. It's nothing to get excited
about, just a little thing Commander M has arranged—
but he wants it to be a surprise."

"It seems unlike him to be bothering over the social
round at a time like this," Lorna responded, unsatisfied.

"Don't be such a worry. It's a pre-Christmas treat for
the wives. Now, I can't say more. You come over as
soon as you can. But get there by eleven—for early
cocktails!" And Ouvry strode off.

Security stopped Lorna at the gates of *Vernon*. "Mrs
Ouvry? Drive straight in, will you, madam? You'll be
directed to your place when you've parked the car."

As a result of the next few hours an extract from the
London Gazette could be quoted as follows:

The King has been graciously pleased to give orders for
the following appointments to the Distinguished Service
Order:

To be Officers of the Distinguished Service Order

Lieutenant-Commander John Garnault Delahaize Ouvry, R.N., Lieutenant-Commander Roger Curzon Lewis, R.N., for great courage and skill in securing and stripping live enemy mines, without regard for their own safety.

His Majesty has also been graciously pleased to approve the following awards for services on the same action:

The Distinguished Service Medal

Chief Petty Officer Charles E. Baldwin; Able Seaman Archibald L. Vearncombe.

Number One was awarded the Distinguished Service Cross.

Before breakfast next morning Lorna propped *The Times* up against the kitchen window-sill, flattened its unfeminine-size pages on the draining-board, and re-lived the exciting events of the day before:

> Today the King paid a visit to the Navy at Portsmouth. He was accompanied during the tour by Admiral Sir William James, Commander-in-Chief. His Majesty first went to H.M.S. *Vernon*, where he was shown German mines and examined with interest the mechanism of these weapons. The Navy's devices for sweeping up the mines and rendering them harmless were fully explained to him.
>
> Before leaving the *Vernon* the King conferred the D.S.O. on Lieutenant-Commander J. G. D. Ouvry, R.N., and Lieutenant-Commander R. C. Lewis, R.N., and the D.S.M. on Chief Petty Officer C. E. Baldwin and Able Seaman A. Vearncombe.
>
> These decorations were awarded "in recognition of the recipients' great courage and skill in rendering safe and ready for inspection enemy mines at great risk of their lives." These officers and men were the experts who voluntarily undertook the risk of dissecting enemy mines.

"You're up early, darling." Ouvry joined her. "In the rush yesterday I forgot to show you the wire Lewis and I got from the Naval Control Service people up at Essex. It says: 'We all at Southend send our congratulations and are even proud the baby was born on our doorstep.'"

"How nice of them, John!"

"Clever bit of writing, too, getting round censorship like that. I couldn't have done it. Now for a quiet week-end."

One day a long time later a fierce storm blew up around the Firth of Forth. Some of the many British deep-laid mines, set to catch any submarines that ventured within, cut loose. Tossed on the tide, they were hurled up the Firth like a pack of wild animals freed of their fetters. Thrown against the inner shore defences by the force of the gale, the first one exploded, shattering steel and concrete, twisting it into useless rubble. Others stampeded on towards the shipping.

Admiralty flashed out a signal to Rosyth: "Pick them up. Destroy them." Baldwin was on hand, so was sent out in a trawler to help get any which were threatening the vessels. One was heading up the Firth straight for a supply-ship.

"I suggest we put out a skiff, sir," the Chief shouted to the skipper, above the roar of the wind. "We'll never get it in otherwise."

"If you think you can handle it, Chief, go ahead, but I don't fancy the job myself."

"I'll do what I can."

The aim was to retrieve the mine and hoist it inboard for subsequent disposal. Oars made little headway in the teeth of the wind-lashed sea. Eventually they roped it and towed it back to the trawler. She was rocking badly by now. The derrick swung over, hooked the mine, lifted it. The haul inboard was hell. The skiff bobbed crazily as Baldwin watched the lift. Half-way in, the trawler tossed. The mine struck her upperworks.

"Look out!" the Chief shouted.

It did not go off. At that moment a sailor swung the mooring-rope in to get a hold on something attached to the mine. Tugging this rope connected to its underside at once made the mine live. The ship rocked over again towards the skiff. The mine swung inboard a second time. A horn hit her side.

Five hundred pounds of high explosive flashed across the Firth. The ship shuddered. The skiff sank. Baldwin was killed.

3

On Land, under Water

WITH the mysteries of the magnetic mine laid bare, two antidotes were soon evolved. As fast as conditions allowed ships of all kinds were girdled with an electric cable to counteract the effect their magnetism would have on a mine. Additionally, an organization set up under Rear-Admiral Wake-Walker produced positive— as opposed to passive—defence against the no-longer-secret weapon. Channels were swept by shallow-draught ships towing long lengths of heavy electric cable astern. Through this cable a current was passed, so that mines might be actuated at a safe distance from the sweepers. All such measures took time, however, and casualties continued. But at least answers were being applied, and activity hummed, instead of frustration. On December 4 the battleship *Nelson* was mined as she entered Loch Ewe, but she was able to make port. The Germans never found this out, remarkably enough.

A week after John Ouvry and his colleagues had been decorated at *Vernon*, and only a month after the actual recovery of the first mine, it was Christmas Day, 1939, and Mr Churchill felt justified in penning an optimistic note from the Admiralty to the Prime Minister:

> Everything is very quiet here, but I thought you would like to know that we have had a marked success against

the magnetic mines. The first two devices for setting them off which we have got into action have both proved effective. It also looks as if the demagnetization of warships and merchant-ships can be accomplished by a simple, speedy, and inexpensive process. We all feel pretty sure that the danger from magnetic mines will soon be out of the way. We are also studying the possible varying forms of this attack—*viz.*, acoustic and supersonic mines. Thirty ardent experts are pursuing these possibilities, but I am not yet able to say that they have found a cure.

Back at *Vernon*, the basic job of finding the mines went on, without which the scientists could not go into action. Blossom bedecked the boughs of the trees lining the *Vernon* roadway. It was the 1st of May, and the sun shone. Ouvry looked out over the harbour, then nearer to hand, at the two old British horn mines flanking the doorway to Mine Design Department. The old Mining School, as it would always be remembered by a lot of them. The 1st of May, the day when the naval caps suddenly blossomed into white. The signal of summer approaching. The little portholes at intervals up the sides of the mining-tank winked in the sun. The phone rang.

"Clacton, you say? We'll know that coastline before we've finished. Very well; I'll pick up Hodges, and we'll make our way up there at once."

Gradually a few more men were being added to the little group which just about now became known as the Enemy Mining Section—E.M.S. for short.

At Clacton the car made for the address given. "Plane must have crashed," Ouvry observed logically, as fragments of the fuselage greeted their gaze. A lone special constable confronted them. "Have you come about the mine, sir?"

"Yes. Could you show it to us, please?" Ouvry asked.

"Well, I could have done three hours ago, sir, but the other naval gentlemen have already been here, you know, and they've made it safe and had it towed away by a breakdown van."

"Well, I'll be——" expostulated Hodges, a two-ringer R.N.V.R.

"Nothing for it but to go over and see them. Where have they gone, did you say?" Ouvry asked.

"Brightlingsea, I think it was they said, sir."

"I call that a pretty piece of cheek!" Ouvry reprimanded Lieutenant-Commanders Lewis and Ryan, who had been responsible for the 'coup.' "How on earth did you do it?"

"You're not the only one who can do this sort of thing, Ouvry, old boy. We thought we'd better show you!"

"Well, let's hear all about it, then, you two rogues!"

"It was like this, John," Lewis started. "Forman, another Wavy Navy boy, like Hodges here, was sent over from Harwich this morning to inspect the damage caused by a German plane which crashed on Clacton last night about 2100—complete with its 'bomb-load.'

"Forman found things more or less as reported, except for a suspicious 'object' near the wreck. The local A.R.P. thought it was the cistern from one of the houses which had been hit, but he recognized it as a magnetic mine, so went off post-haste to phone you.

"Meanwhile Ryan rang me from Admiralty to say he was coming to have a look, so I met him at Wivenhoe and drove him over. Forman was actually away phoning you when we got there—and by the time he got back it was all over!

"The local paper snapped us in our shirt-sleeves re-plenishing our thirst direct out of beer-bottles, but their pictures were censored, luckily."

"What luck you've had all the way through! Now, how about the mine?" Ouvry asked anxiously.

"We handled the bomb-fuse as per your instructions. The mine must have been thrown clear when the plane crashed. Anyway, the impact was not enough to fire the fuse. But that's enough about mines for a little while. We'll give you a good feed now you're here."

After their car-trip from Portsmouth the *Vernon* party were positively peckish, and fell upon the dainties laid before them—plovers' eggs which Lewis had collected locally the previous week.

When Lewis came to write out his report of the Clacton affair it included several significant points. First, that the bomb-fuse was afterwards discovered by *Vernon* scientists to have been in a highly dangerous state, near to firing. Second, that the mine was a new magnetic type—with blue polarity—which was luckily dissected and countered before the Germans laid large quantities. Third, a mild complaint that the *Vernon* party had eaten an overlarge proportion of his precious plovers' eggs!

The Admiralty released the news, especially for German ears, that the plane's bomb-load, or mine-load, had exploded. In fact, Britain had her first magnetic mine of this particular type—without the enemy's knowing it.

To win the War the great thing was to keep one jump ahead all the time. Our own new non-contact mines were being put into service at top priority. And the campaign against enemy mines continued unabated. All the latest types were worth their weight in gold, even though they averaged something approaching a ton each. But rare were the times when they could be counted on to be presented on a platter, as at Clacton. More often, quite naturally, they would be found among their natural habitat, under water.

Here arose a major snag which *Vernon* had already by this time overcome in theory. As a mine was taken from deeper into shallower water, and eventually out of it altogether, the pressure was released on the bomb-fuse, and the mine was thus apt to fire. Accordingly a new safety fitting was evolved to go over the fuse as a mine was brought ashore, to retain the pressure, and so prevent its loss by firing. By the beginning of June trials were complete on this gadget. Whether it would work in practice remained to be seen. The wait was not long.

During the first week of June attempts were being made to evacuate part of the sorely tried British Expeditionary Force from Saint-Valéry by a diversity of shipping rushed to the scene. The Germans assumed that Poole Harbour would be the natural goal of many of the vessels making the getaway, so mines were laid in the approaches to this vital harbour to try to catch the ships as they came home to 'safety.'

On the morning of June 6 the waters around the Hampshire and Dorset coast were shimmering in early-summer sun. And out of this sun the look-out aboard H.M.S. *Saltburn* saw an enemy aircraft drop a mine off Poole Bar buoy. The ship flashed a signal to F.O.I.C., Portland, reporting: "Aircraft-laid mine slightly out of the main channel." The news was at once communicated to *Vernon*, who requested approval for recovering it. An area of two cables had to be reserved around the estimated location of the mine. This could be guaranteed only as it was out of the channel.

Lieutenant-Commander Anderson organized a plan of attack. Echo-sounding ships were to examine the area to try to locate the mine. Divers standing by would be ready to go down and look at any objects reflecting the 'ping' of the echo-sounder. Then, when the mine was found, a specially trained diver would descend to render it safe under water—after which it could be dragged ashore and later examined at *Vernon*.

Two days elapsed. The echo-sounding yachts *Esmeralda* and *Sir Sydney* arrived at Poole to commence operations under Lieutenant-Commander Macmillan, R.N.R. A mobile diving unit from *Excellent* reassembled. Six separate contacts on the echo-sounder were investigated the same day, but the divers found only ledges of rock. Strong tides made diving difficult, but no doubt existed that the mine had not yet come to light. The following day, June 9, three further contacts again yielded nothing. At this juncture R.N.O., Poole, sent a signal to suspend operations and sail the yachts back to base at Portsmouth. This order was obeyed, although *Esmeralda* had located still three more suspects which the intention was to investigate.

Three days passed. Fresh orders came through: "Resume operations." So *Esmeralda* and *Sir Sydney* set off again, retracing their course. Gosport, a row of deserted beach-huts, discoloured. Lee-on-Solent, the tall white tower already a favourite naval landmark for incoming sailors. Ships on the slipway at East Cowes. Southampton Water running inland to the great passenger port. Past the Needles, each rock a little lower than the one before, till they vanish into the June-blue water. Away to the south Tennyson's Down, on the Island. No poetic mission, this, but for a cause that the bard would have taken to his heart. Christchurch, and the Priory grey with the dignity of age. So to Boscombe, then Bournemouth. *Esmeralda* and *Sir Sydney* clung close to the shore. Macmillan could see the groups of holiday-makers—even in this fateful summer of 1940. On to Sandbanks the two trim little vessels sailed, past that slender strip of nature and artifice, half enclosing the harbour of Poole. The diving unit again stood at the ready; and on the 13th the luck changed.

Macmillan paced his bridge all forenoon. Then at 1517 one of the divers following up a previous contact reported a mine directly below *Esmeralda*. From the description it was clearly a German magnetic of the latest type, so had to be salved. It lay in seven fathoms at an angle of about thirty degrees to the bottom, swinging gently on the ebb tide—nearly a quarter of a mile from the position at which it was reported to have dropped. Rather an alarming thought: that mines might stroll over the sea-bed to considerable lengths. It was secured, the position marked by a buoy, and a signal sent to *Vernon*. Number One was dispatched to take charge of the actual salvage, assisted by a group of *Vernon* divers trained in rendering mines safe. The party arrived on the 14th.

Diver R. G. Tawn, able seaman, descended to seven fathoms. He found the mine flat on the bottom, darkly visible through the grey-green luminosity. Its lifting-lug was on top. Fifteen hundred pounds of high explosive lay leashed at his elbows as he moved slowly,

E

sluggishly, in his diving-suit around its shell. Uncomfortably close. But there was not a lot to choose between being a matter of inches from it and seven fathoms, as the *Esmeralda* was, swaying lazily at anchor.

Up aloft a great calm had come down on the crew. "I hate this damned waiting, Number One," Macmillan burst out at last. "Tawn's got the worst job, but we're all in a delicate position, to put it mildly."

A slight splash against the side.

"Talking about sitting on a hornet's nest," agreed the First Lieutenant. "I'd far rather be down there than hanging about here. At least it wouldn't all seem so blessed ghostly."

Forty-two feet below them Tawn got the new safety "motor horn" fitting firmly in his hand. He felt the bomb-fuse with studied care. The gentle swell of the sea made each move more difficult, dangerous. Complete control over movement was impossible. He screwed the horn on to the fuse. Its pressure kept up to ten pounds, and it was fitted with a tap. The mine should have been safe to beach, but he had suggested removing the fuse down there to save two separate operations. So, having screwed the motor horn on, he could safely remove the whole thing from the mine, which he did. Grabbing it in his left hand, he attached it to a line with his right, gave a tug on the line, and the contrivance was hauled up to the surface, when the fuse was unfitted from its protector.

"I've been considering where is the most convenient spot to beach the mine," Macmillan told Number One, "and I think that Studland Bay is about the best bet, if you agree. We'll tow it until we can pass warps ashore."

"That's your department, sir," Number One responded.

"I wouldn't dream of doing otherwise than agree, so let's get cracking."

Sir Sydney searched the run into the beach for obstructions. Then a 120-fathom tow-line was fixed to the mine, and the entire operation transferred to a small, open Poole fishing-boat, which proceeded to tow it inshore. For about two hundred yards the mine travelled comfortably. It came along two hundred and forty yards astern.

"Do you think she's going to do it?" Number One asked anxiously. But before Macmillan had time to consider the question they were flung off their feet: the frail-looking little craft was rocked by a thunderous roar which upswept gallon upon gallon of swirling spray into the summer air. A few seconds later a glass-smooth circle of water took its place at sea-level. The mine had fired.

Back at base Number One was commiseratory. "Never mind, Tawn; you were the first bloke to work on an enemy mine under water. And in confidence I'll tell you that you haven't heard the last of it."

"Thanks, sir, but it's a pity to have got it just so far—and no farther."

"Quite agree, but better it went off then than a couple of hours earlier, eh?"

"Lord! I never thought of that!"

The day was not wasted, for out of it came the birth of interesting ideas for improving methods of recovering mines, several of which were later adopted. And to Diver Tawn Number One was as good as his word. A recommendation went through the usual channels—on the surface this time—and soon afterwards he was wearing the ribbon of the D.S.M.

4

Tragedy

FRANCE fell. Le quatorze juillet a tragic travesty. And as August dawned another tragedy was to plunge the *Vernon* into sharp shadow. The Battle of Britain was getting into its stride. Invasion rumours were rife. Lord Haw-Haw's infuriatingly equable and patronizing perorations infiltrated into Britain via the air. The Luftwaffe was not to get across so easily. And while the famous Few were about to live their finest hour the Navy's Few toiled on. Two or three rounds had been won. More must be fought before the *Vernon* victory.

The Garden of England—or Hell's Corner. This was the setting for the start of the story. Ted Pearson, driver of a local train from Chatham to Margate, was looking straight ahead about 1500 on Saturday, August 3. It was hot, and one of those mists drifted in from the Channel, crossing the line a mile or two farther on.

This time last year I'd have been batting on the green, he thought. Now everything has changed. It doesn't seem to matter much whether I ever make my century. Each season I was sure I'd get it by August. But now . . . none of the boys are about any more. If they're not away they're working at week-ends, like me. Be glad to get home to-night. Hope there's no trouble.

As he mused his head nodded slightly to the rhythm

of train over track . . . train over track . . . hope I get back.

Above the beat the siren sounded over towards Birchington. Ted glanced around the skies. The mist was thickening now. Ack-ack cracked into action. A pause. Then gossamer puffs in the August air. He could not see what they were aiming at, but they must have been near the target, for the next thing he was aware of was a mine billowing down by parachute a little ahead and to the left of the track. The heat-haze hung thicker over the ground. He lost sight of it. He jammed on the brakes. The train screeched to a halt. Ted peered through the mist, but could not catch a glimpse of it again. Can't do anything here, he thought. I'd better run it on to the next station. A platelayer sent to investigate the incident traced the mine and confirmed the position. The Admiralty received the report and signalled *Vernon*: "Mine buried in field by Minnis Bay, near Birchington, Kent."

Commander G. Thistleton-Smith was 'on board' when the message was received. He had succeeded Sayer in January as Commander M. He rang for a duty Wren.

"Ask Lieutenant Hodges to come in and see me, will you?"

Portsmouth was quiet as he waited for Hodges; most people were asleep. He looked at his watch: 2330.

"Ah, Hodges, there's a job for you in Kent. These things always seem to happen on duty week-ends, don't they? Take Chief Wheeler with you. I've arranged for a car at 0700 from Dockyard. Seems to be a standard mine, so you shouldn't have too much trouble. But take care of yourself. You never know with Jerry; it's high time he switched to something else unpleasant. The only thing here is that it's buried in the good Kentish earth."

"That'll be all right, sir. We'll find a way." And, quoting a favourite tag: "The impossible takes a little longer, though, of course!" Lieutenant Hodges, R.N.V.R., was a modest master at Winchester College in peace-time.

"As far as I can see, there's nothing else to tell you. I understand there was quite a thick mist hovering over the land a little, as well as the sea, and the pilot must have mistaken his position and thought he was dropping it into the drink. Whereas, in fact, he seems to have been a quarter of a mile inland. Not much, I suppose, really."

It was nearly midnight. The Wren reappeared.

"Another signal from Admiralty, sir, about the Kent mine."

"Well, you'd better wait a second, Hodges, while we see what it says." He unfolded the tissue-thin sheet. "Nothing much to add. More planes have been laying inshore near Birchington only an hour ago, so this one of yours must just be one of the batch reported earlier in the same area."

"Blast the Dockyard, Chief! These cars have never yet been known to be on time. Here we are, rarin' to go at 0730, and not a sign of transport."

"Aye, sir, they'd miss the boat every time if they had to be casting off at the times they're supposed to pick people up."

As the car swung through *Vernon* gates and in towards the main block the sirens of the city wailed welcome to

Sunday morning, August 4, 1940—the twenty-sixth anniversary of the outbreak of the First World War.

"Pretty poor start, Chief. Now we'll have to wait again."

It was 0830 when they finally left. The driver was an elderly man, inscrutable, imperturbable.

"As we're an hour and a half late, driver, do be a good fellow and step on it, will you?" pleaded Hodges. But to no avail. Never did he top forty, so that by the time they arrived a party from near-by Chatham torpedo school, under a Lieutenant West, were already digging themselves in and proposing to dig the mine out.

Perfectly perpendicular it was, embedded, with a bare bottom all that was visible. The rest lay underground.

"I've been studying the lie of the land, Hodges, and I suggest we haul it out by tractor," West said, with the obvious optimism of the very eager.

"I'm not too keen on the idea, but we'll give it a try," acquiesced Hodges, conscious of feeling slightly like a trespasser on their home territory.

From early afternoon through to late evening three prolonged attempts were made along these lines. In the heat of the day a mud-spattered red tractor nearly burst its entrails trying to haul the thing clear. Nothing budged. Attempt number two was prefaced by a token loosening of the soil round the mine, followed by an equally unsuccessful heave. Finally more digging revealed correspondingly more mine, and another tractor was conscripted—still to no avail. The long tow-rope needed had to be run across the railway-line, moreover, which considerably complicated and extended operations.

"I'd think you'd better have a shot at it to-morrow, Hodges," West conceded.

Next day, August 5, Hodges took over. The earth was thoroughly dug, in true Mr Middleton style; a ramp cut; rollers positioned for the tow-rope; and the mine slid easily out.

Hodges, West, and Wheeler tackled it.

"It's a type C," pronounced Hodges. "You can help me with the detonator, if you will, West." The other Lieutenant needed no second bidding. Whoever the man handling these mines, the inevitable thrill swept over him as he realized that he was dicing with death. The instructions they had to follow were explicit, staid, and intended to ensure as high a degree of safety as was humanly possible—but the unknown element always existed, to bring a lump to the throat of hardened veterans.

"I'm going to use the new safety horn," Hodges told West. "If Tawn could manage it forty feet under Poole Harbour I ought to be able to work the thing here, unless I'm a damn fool." With it the bomb-fuse came out safely. "Ouvry didn't have anything like this at Shoeburyness, you know," he went on. "In fact, he didn't have a thing to go on, just blind faith, if you ask me— plus a shrewd mind and gallons of guts." Hodges got the primer out, and yet another mine was written off as safe.

"My God, almost 1400 already! If we're going to get back to Pompey to-night we'd better be pushing off. We'll have to leave the arming-clock in the thing, anyway. There's no box to pack it in, and it'll all take more time." At 1500 Wheeler was able to report "All aboard, sir," and the three-ton, 20-m.p.h. vehicle moved off westward, waved away by West and his matelots. Although bearing the meagre mileage limit on its flank, the lorry made better time back to *Vernon* than the Dockyard car's effort the morning before. It had been a crowded thirty-six hours, thought Hodges; I'll be glad to get some sleep. By 2200 the mine was safely stowed away in *Vernon*, tucked up for the night in the mining-shed. Hodges slept soundly.

Next morning after breakfast a "yellow" air-raid warning sounded in *Vernon*, and Hodges made his way over to the mining-shed to recover the clock in case the mine had to be ditched. Regulations were that on receipt of a "red" warning—imminent danger, instead of a general alarm—all live mines had to be dropped into the harbour at once. The reason was obvious. With a few three-quarter-ton mines languishing on the base, half the place might be blown to bits by a single incendiary. The "red" did not come, but by the time Hodges reached the mining-shed Number One and his working party had already started dismantling and were about to tackle the rear door of the mine—the main cover which had to be undone before the major task of stripping for inspection could be carried out.

"Nothing for you to do, Hodges, but I tell you what —Lieutenant-Commander Forest here, of the United States Navy, is anxious for a visit to Priddy's Hard, so I'd be glad if you could spare an hour or two and show him round over there."

"I'd be right glad if you could do that for me, Lieutenant," chipped in Forest. "I reckon it'd be a real education on explosives over there from what your First Lieutenant has been telling me. Come in mighty handy when we're with you in this goddam war."

"Well, Number One, if you're sure you can handle

things here I'd be glad to participate in a bit of Anglo-American co-operation. Makes us feel a little less cut off to have you over."

Hodges led Forest away up to Commander M's room.

"I'm sure it will be quite in order for you to go straight over to the Hard," the Commander confirmed, "but I'll just put a call through to make certain. You did a nice job on the Birchington mine, Hodges. By the way, you've seen Number One, I take it. He'll cope with the routine stripping. It'll be a change for him from yanking out detonators. Sorry, Forest—no pun intended! Anyway, I'm snowed under here with piles of papers, so I shan't go down till they've finished in the shed. If the number of Admiralty Fleet Orders is in direct proportion to the power of the Navy we ought to be sweeping the board with the whole world by now! Still, I suppose we mustn't grumble."

Thistleton-Smith (M) had his word with Priddy's Hard, and motioned *au revoir* to the two of them as another call came through as soon as he had put the receiver down. The "yellow" warning cleared to "white." Hodges and Forest walked down to the *Vernon's* Marlborough Pier and cast off in the *Skimming Dish*, a light harbour craft, which set her bows up-harbour for Priddy's Hard. M replaced his receiver again, took up his pen. The *Skimming Dish* sounded a short defiant toot to the near-by warships. M scrawled his initials, G.T.-S., across a document.

The last nut was loosened from the rear door of the mine. Petty Officer Fletcher held the door in his hands. The suction of the rubber jointing-band between it and the main body yielded a bit. A sudden whirring sound. A blinding flash. A roar. Then blank.

Hodges and Forest looked up quickly to see the roof blown out of the mining-shed. M's window shook. He thought it was a bomb in the city. Lieutenant Hight was with him. Both looked out of the windows. A sailor rushed in. "There's been an explosion, sir." An ambulance moved across to the shed. M and Hight ran over, too.

An incredible sight. Blackened men, brutally burned, were being helped out by the south door. The officers rushed round to the north end. The shed was a shambles. The mine hurled against the office in the corner. The sky gaping through the roof. Glass—and blood. A contorted figure flung into a corner. A sailor collecting charred remains . . . putting them on a trolley. A leg. Mr Cook, commissioned gunner, was dying before their eyes. No one could save him. Little was left of Fletcher.

They did what they could to help. But there was not very much. After a short while Rear-Admiral Egerton, Captain of *Vernon*, came up beside M. He spoke softly. "What a terrible thing! We must see that nothing like it ever happens again. Somehow or other."

M did not know quite how long elapsed. Hight was still with him. "Did you see Number One, Hight? He wasn't reported killed?"

"I asked about him just now, sir. No one seems to know quite, not at the moment. One of the S.B.A.'s said he might be in the Sick Bay. Shall we go over there now?"

"Yes." M had to know about Number One. But he no longer ran. Whatever had happened to him, he could not do anything. But he could—and did—move heaven and earth to see that the men he had under him never looked like those ashen faces engraved on his brain.

Thistleton-Smith came to the Lieutenant in the last bunk of the Sick Bay. He was badly burned and suffering from shock. Presently he opened his eyes. His lips parted a fraction. A suggestion of a smile passed between them. Then a line broke over his forehead. He whispered, "What happened, sir? I was standing behind Fletcher. He undid the nut. Then . . . a flash. Was it bad?"

"Don't talk any more, old man. You must keep quiet. You got some nasty burns. It's a miracle you're alive. But you are—and you'll get well. If you hadn't been behind Fletcher at that moment . . ."

"He's dead?"

"I'm afraid so. And Cook and four others. Precious lives lost. But just relax. We need you back again, so concentrate on that, and I'll do my best to get things shipshape to meet anything Jerry lets us have. He's not going to get away with this. We'll go on getting his stuff, and we won't get caught like this again. Try not to dwell on it. It's over now. Nothing can alter it."

Number One nodded. He did not speak. The two men looked at each other for a moment, then M left.

The Commander walked back towards his office. He paused at the old sliding doors of the mining-shed, and looked in. A working-party had tidied up the debris. The sun still shone through the roof. Pulleys hung dangling from the steel girders. Sheets of corrugated iron had been loosened from the 'gable' wall over the doors. The little office in the corner stood empty. The whole place had been cleared for photography and investigation. He looked over at the mine. The rear door lay near by, with its three fins, each set at 120 degrees to the others. Bits of tangled metal lay all around. The sailors had been told to leave them. One portion of the rim of the mine was badly buckled. It was obvious that a special charge had been inserted to go off and destroy the mine, or at least its working parts, if the rear door were removed. Why? What did the Germans want to conceal? The only compensation he could think of at that moment was that Ouvry had not been killed at Shoeburyness by something similar.

The civilian scientific section collected all the bits and pieces, worked day and night, as in the previous November, and reconstructed the mechanism down to the last detail—despite the explosion. Matter is indestructible: the Germans had neglected this basic scientific postulation. Or perhaps had counted on the whole mine going up, too. That would have been a major tragedy which would have multiplied the loss of life tenfold. As it was, the scientists solved the mystery once more—an electrically fired charge whose circuit was completed by the withdrawal of a stud attached to the rear door. And the secret that the explosion was meant to guard—a "clicker" delay mechanism which the Germans were incorporating to complicate minesweeping. The object was for the sweeper to actuate the magnetic firing circuit out of range of the vessel, as a result of which the mine did not fire at once, but clicked one of six delays. This prevented the mine actually exploding until all the clicks had happened, when the sixth ship of a convoy would fire the thing, or the channel be swept up five times without wasting the mine. To be effective, however, this had to remain secret, and if the *Vernon* tragedy caused loss of life it also brought this new development to light.

From August 6 onward, all mines recovered were to be taken to a remote spot set in the South Downs, where the effect of any similar accidents would not be so serious as in the congested *Vernon* areas. The incorporation of "prevention-of-stripping" equipment—the fatal small charge at *Vernon*—also meant that two new approaches became imperative. First, a certain treatment was evolved which enabled *Vernon* to estimate more accurately exactly what they were up against—a technique that is still secret to-day. Second, a remote-controlled, pneumatic non-magnetic trepanning machine was provided to cut a hole in the aluminium alloy casing of the mine, so that any trickery could be got at without opening the obvious joints—and from a distance.

On August 15 Ouvry became officer in charge of the Enemy Mining Section. And on the very next morning, only ten days after the *Vernon* affair, the call came for the equipment which had been rushed into production. The ensuing episode was to rank as one of the most fantastic of all time. It began just after midnight on August 17.

5

A Crime is Conquered

A THICK ground mist settled over the little community of North Boarhunt on the night of August 16–17. The pub closed its doors. The villagers wended their slightly unsteady way home, shivering in the cool air. The village nestles near Southwick, just behind Portsdown Hill, not far from Portsmouth. The duty watch of the Home Guard, defiantly sporting their "H20" shoulder-flashes, and not much else, prepared to face another night. Invasion was an imminent possibility. They could do little but wait for it this night, though; no sky was to be scanned. The mist induced a sense of oppression, enclosure, despite the chill.

At 0014 the warning went—a nightmarish wail that added to the mystery. All continued quiet. Then at 0020 the unmistakable drone of an enemy plane. Round and round it circled, out of sight, very much in sound. An ominous, insistent note quivering through the veil.

"Wonder what he's up to?"

"Never tell with these Jerries. Perhaps he's lost his way. Nothing here at Boarhunt worth bombing."

The noise of the engine began to fade.

"Must have given up and gone home."

The next second a green flash lit up the near-by field. The mist stirred in its sleep. And a muffled explosion reached their ears. The two Home Guards hurried over to the low meadow. Torches pierced the gloom. Soon they saw the source of the outburst. Parts of a mine still smouldered in the field. A green silk parachute lay draped over a hedge.

"Not much of an explosion for its size. Shouldn't go near it if I were you, Tom. May still be some to go off."

"We'd better go and report it quick."

The two stalwarts returned to the little H.G. post and phoned the local headquarters, who passed the information on to C.-in-C., Portsmouth.

Commander Thistleton-Smith had had a hectic ten days since the *Vernon* accident. The daylight raids were intensifying. Now he slept soundly in his little room at the Red Lion Hotel, Petersfield, out in the country. The phone awoke him at 0230.

"Commander M? It's duty officer, C.-in-C., here, sir. I've been instructed to tell you that a parachute mine has been dropped near Bere Farm, North Boarhunt. Within the last couple of hours it was, sir. Our orders are that *Vernon* has to handle these things. That's right, isn't it, sir?" The junior officer suddenly wondered if he had done his duty by disturbing a three-ringer at an hour like this.

"Quite right," M reassured him, not completely out of his slumber.

"One other point, sir. The Home Guards who saw the flash and heard it go off say that the explosion was only slight."

"Very well. Boarhunt's not far from here, so I'll pop down in my car as soon as it's light. What was the name of the farm again? Bere? You might ring through to

Vernon early A.M., please, and let them know that I may be a little late getting in."

While M got another couple of hours' sleep the mist was clearing. His alarm rang at 0430. He pressed a flat palm down to stop it. He dressed quickly, got the car out of the garages, converted from old coaching stables. Quietly, by 0500, he let it run down the slight slope on to the main road, slipped it into gear, and headed south-south-west. The cobbled market square of Petersfield lay still in an August dawn. It was the magic moment of clear early morning. Dew glistened on the Downs. A late-summer nip freshened the air. Pale pink clouds, gossamer-and-gauze-like, wisped in the blue.

After a few wrong turnings down narrow Hampshire lanes M saw the first soul of the day, a grocer's boy up early polishing his delivery cycle. "Excuse me, sonny, but can you tell me if I'm anywhere near Bere Farm?"

"Oh, it's the parachute mine you're looking for, is it, sir? Why, that be just down the next lane!"

The news had travelled fast. How it could have done was hard to comprehend—but it had. Negotiating another bend, tortuously and with the heavy hedges nearly invading the car, M spied the constable guarding the scene.

"Mornin', sir."

"Hello, there. Glad to see you. I've come to take a look at the mine, officer. Can we move on?"

"Certainly, sir; come along down. I'll have to see your pass first, though—if you don't mind me asking."

"Why, of course not. Very proper of you, too."

The pair dropped down to the low meadow. M badly

F

wanted to be able to deal with the thing himself, but as soon as he saw it his hopes faded. It all seemed to be in bits. The two of them walked round it in silence for a minute, M trying to piece together in his mind what could have occurred. At first he thought it had partially exploded. But the end of the mine carrying the detonator and primer was still intact. And there was no crater— only a small circle of burnt grass. Surrounding that the ground was covered with pieces of explosive. Clearly there had been some sort of explosion. The Home Guard and the folk at the farm had heard that. But what had exploded—and why? These were the questions troubling M as he scrutinized the remains.

A few yards off lay a heavy cylinder. A deposit of yellow explosive on its exterior revealed that it had been fitted into the main charge. It looked like a primer. If it were, why had it not gone off? Little bits of mangled metal lay scattered over a couple of acres. In the next field M found the usual tail-cap of the mine.

"Thanks, constable. I'm going back to *Vernon*, and some one will be back here later in the day."

"Very well, sir. I'll look after it till then. Hope nothing else goes off in the meantime."

"So do I. But I think you're safe enough. Keep away from it, anyway. There's something a bit fishy about it all. Things aren't just as they should be."

M got down to *Vernon* for a late breakfast in the mess. He left a message at the door to be called as soon as Ouvry arrived. A steward came over as he was about to spread jelly marmalade on toast. "Lieutenant-Commander Ouvry has just come aboard, sir. You wanted to know." Three-quarters of a slice of succulent toast went despondently uneaten. M marched purposefully over to see Ouvry, and told him all about it, repeating the observation he had made to the law at sunrise. "I think you'll agree with me when you see it that something's rotten in the state of Boarhunt. Apart from the detonator and primer being still unexploded, and that second primer thrown clear, why was the mine dropped so far inland, anyway? There's a possibility, I suppose, that the pilot was trying to place one near the back of the harbour. From the air Boarhunt's probably only a mile or two away from Porchester, which is about the limit of the harbour."

"It's possible," Ouvry agreed, "but not too probable, although the mist must have confused the issue—for him as well as for us. It could have looked like water from the air."

M nodded, but neither of them was really convinced.

"Anyway, I'll run up there, sir, and see what I can find."

"Keep your wits about you. I've got a funny feeling about this one, and we can't afford to lose you."

By 1030 Ouvry was at Bere Farm. Carefully he extracted the main detonator and primer. The sun shone down on a sylvan scene. Strange day to be tinkering with this, he thought—and a strange setting too. War and peace. Tolstoy at North Boarhunt. Ouvry found no bomb-fuse. He walked over to the farm, and with the willing help of the farmer scoured the field for all the particles. Everything was loaded on to a lorry, and the party was back at *Vernon* in record time—by noon. The operation on site had taken only an hour.

"Come down into the mining-shed," Ouvry asked M. "We're just finishing reconstructing the crime, as it

were." Walden[1] was there too. In the shed they came
to the conclusion that there had obviously been an electrical booby-trap, similar to the *Vernon* mine, set to
operate when the rear door came off. But it became
clear too that the cylindrical charge, a primer, which
Thistleton-Smith had found near the mine was the
charge for this trap. The cylinder seemed to have fitted
into a central hole in the rear end of the main charge.
If this was so a second auxiliary charge had actually
fired, and could not have been in contact with the main
charge. And a third charge must have been fitted which
actually exploded by accident on hitting the ground.
Not only was the bomb-fuse missing—its hole was filled
up with the main explosive charge. But by far the most
pertinent point of all was that there was no clock or
magnetic unit in the mine.

"There's only one thing to conclude from this," M
spoke gravely. "The Huns are prepared to go to any
lengths to stop us discovering the secrets of their circuits.
We're all agreed on that. But there's nothing here to
suggest that this is a real mine—or could ever blow up a
ship. In fact, it's not a mine at all. It all adds up. *The
thing has been planted ashore with the explicit intention of
killing as many of us as possible, and scaring the rest from
ever going near one again.*"

"It certainly looks like that," said Ouvry. "What
amazing lengths to resort to! A triple booby-trap!"

"Not so amazing really. They know we're winning our
particular part of the War, and they've got to start something desperate. But we won't be put off by this sort of
stuff. Our new technique will help, and the trepanning
machine will be ready in a day or two. From now on no

[1] Leonard Walden was a civilian scientist attached to *Vernon*.

undue risks, mind you. It's all going to be strictly scientific."

It was nearly 1300. One or two fitters were finishing their sandwiches, sitting on empty mine-shells. The phone sounded from the office in the corner. The foreman stopped counting his wage-packet, answered it, then called over: "It's for you, Commander."

Thistleton-Smith walked over the floor where the six men had been killed on the 6th. "M speaking. What's that? Another one laid inland? At Piddlehinton. Where on earth's that? Near Portland, eh? Right; thanks very much. We're all ready for it this time."

Then to Ouvry and the others: "A second specimen, gentlemen, somewhere behind Portland. That was F.O.I.C., Portland, on the line. It's beginning to make sense. To be sure, they've dropped one near Pompey and another by Portland—the two premier naval bases on the south coast—where they reckon they're bound to catch us."

Ouvry stayed at *Vernon* this time. M arranged to drive Anderson and Walden down to Piddlehinton the following morning, Saturday. He signalled Woolwich for further equipment to help them, and the new cutting machine was promised for a week hence. The National Physical Laboratory at Teddington, where it was being made, were encouraged to produce it in forty-eight hours instead. The N.P.L. were not used to such pressure!

For once there was no tearing hurry. They had made up their minds to take their time. The lie of the land could be explored on Saturday, and the necessary machines would then arrive soon afterwards. Portsmouth and Southampton both came in for air-raids during the forenoon. The trio reached Lyndhurst, in the green depths of the New Forest. The raids were behind them.

"Where was the place they mentioned, sir?" Anderson asked.

"Piddlehinton's the name. It's in that stretch of country—surely you know it?—the lovely land of Piddles and Wallops, Anderson." M half turned his head from the driving-wheel in reply.

Finally they found the place. As at Boarhunt, the local constable had taken complete control of the proceedings. Here his name, appropriate to the nautical nature of surveillance of a sea-mine, was P.C. Fish. They knocked on his front door about mid-afternoon. Fish asked them in for a minute or two while he collected his coat and helmet, and told the brief details of the raid.

"It was dropped in the very early hours of yesterday morning," Fish revealed.

"What was the weather like?" M demanded quickly.

"Fine. Quite fine, sir, with a full moon and a clear sky. The plane came over fairly high from the south, dropped the mine almost immediately, and made off the way it came."

"How far inland are you exactly here, constable?"

"Well, I reckon it's all of ten miles from Weymouth, so the pilot must have been a tidy way off his course, mustn't he?"

"Perhaps," M replied slowly, "and perhaps not."

They elicited further information that the nearest house was a mile from the position the mine dropped, and the nearest military objective a couple of miles or more.

"Will you take us over to see it now, please? You can come in the car. We've room for one more."

The constable lowered his helmeted head with elaborate caution and showed them the way. The mine lay undamaged, sitting pretty, unexploded, on the slope of a grassy field a mile and a half from Piddlehinton. The setting was one of those rather steep and narrow valleys so typical of Wessex, splitting up the high plains of Wiltshire and Dorset. The four of them seemed miles from anywhere. Stumbling down the steep hillside, M panted, "Funny finding a mine here. I've got exactly the same feeling I had yesterday morning. This second one in the same sort of surroundings is just too much to swallow. There's no doubt it's been planted."

A section of the local soldiery guarded the mine, while also maintaining a respectful distance. It had landed near the summit of the slope and rolled down quite a way before being stopped. The parachute was still attached.

"Looks like a type D. Shape and size are the same," M observed. They took a closer peep. The normal mechanism for releasing the primer and the plate over the detonator were both visible, but no place could be found for fitting either a clock or a bomb-fuse. In this respect the shell differed from the standard they were well used to by this time. They advanced cautiously on it, and listened, rapt, for any ticking. The afternoon wore on. All that came to them was the drowsy murmur of insects on the summer air, with an occasional lark-song.

The mine was photographed and rolled over, to see the other side. "The thing's rolled so far already another turn or two can't hurt," M said logically. And he was right. "Now we'd better wait for the rest of our equipment."

"It seems a shame to do that, sir, when the detonator and primer are normal. Can't I whip them out? If there are any booby-traps I think it's a safe bet they'll be somewhere less obvious." Anderson pleaded very persuasively.

"If you really want to—go ahead, then."

They came out without mishap. All three men breathed a little more freely. "I've got to shove off now," M told them, "but no risks, you understand? Your toys will be along soon, and you can do it all more or less safely then." He was speaking comparatively, of course. M left about 1800.

The next day the new equipment rolled up, and Anderson and Walden got to work. The apparatus was still a trifle imperfect, however, and they decided that expert interpretation was wanted of their findings.

"I'll pop back to *Vernon* to-morrow," Anderson suggested to Walden. "What is it to-day? I've lost all count of time these days. You can get the cutter ready for us when we get back. At this rate it looks like another week-end down the drain, doesn't it? Of course, that's why we find it so hard to keep a tab on time. All the weeks are running into one another. No blessed five-day week—more's the shame."

On Thursday Anderson was back at Piddlehinton. "I've had a conflab with M," he told Walden, "and we're going to try out the trepanner. If we can cut a four-inch hole out at the end of the battery the leads going away to the electrically fired auxiliary charge can be cut. It'll mean getting my hand in a four-inch diameter, but that shouldn't be impossible."

The attempt was short-lived, however, for the cutter

failed to work properly, and the supply of compressed air needed to operate it soon became exhausted, anyway. The day was not wasted, though, for the other apparatus was proving useful. M decided to join the party once more on the next day, Friday. When he arrived Walden had been working on the cutter most of the night and was unshaven. Anderson had just got back from a detailed scouring mission over Dorset for more compressed air. They had been joined by a small working-party, including Chief Petty Officer Thorns. Now they were ready for a full-scale onslaught.

The cutter was made of non-magnetic metal, and clamped on to the circumference of the mine-shell. A mass of cogs, it still looked somehow slightly unscientific. Friday, August 23, six days after they saw Piddlehinton, the work began in earnest. It was the first time a mine had been tackled by remote control. "All they'll need soon is a lot of robots," Anderson volunteered. This was scarcely sufficiently dangerous for the man. Yet the old excitement was there just the same, if he were to admit it.

The soldiers had dug a little slit-trench shelter in the neighbouring field. They retired into this after making final adjustments to the cutter. A twin flex trailed along after them to the main switch.

"All comfortable?" M asked. "Right, then, let's start it turning."

Over the summer air floated the sustained high wail of the cutter. Non-magnetic tool into shell of magnetic mine. On and on it went. Walden switched off. They waited five minutes for a safety margin, then advanced over the stile. "Still a long way to go," Anderson announced. Back they trooped. Over the stile. Into the trench. On went the switch. Up started the wail. This was repeated several times more. The day waned into evening. The sun dropped behind the hills. The fifth time the wail started as usual. They had got used to it by now. Then a moment of triumph. The note of the drill changed. It was through—partially, anyway. They could hardly wait the five minutes. The cutter had done its work on one side. "I'll finish it off with a hacksaw," Walden offered enthusiastically.

"Careful not to poke the end too far down, then," M warned.

"I won't."

The circular metal disc was nearly cut neatly through all round. They all peered at it eagerly, keyed to a fine degree of intensity.

"Can you smell anything?" Walden said suddenly.

M and Anderson sniffed. "Yes, my God; yes, you're right! What is it?"

"Pitch," Walden decided.

"And it's getting worse," M added.

They turned round rapidly, and as they did so M was conscious of puffs of smoke pouring out of his jacket pocket! He had left his pipe in there alight. It was a good blaze, and the lining was no more.

The saw finished off the job. The hole proved to be well positioned, half over the end of the battery, half over a little compartment. But the disc would not come right away from the battery, so Walden cut across it as best he could by boring small holes and cutting through the bits between with his trusty—and rather rusty— hacksaw-blade. Finally the disc snapped off, and there were the leads from the battery all ready to be cut and insulated. A hand and a tool in the hole, and that was one of the booby-traps out of the way. M felt pretty sure that they had isolated the primer in the rear end of the charge, so they were left with a separate explosive charge in the rear compartment—mechanically fired, instead of electrically. And no guidance as how best to tackle it. Moreover, it was near the ribbed rear end, awkward for the cutter to be clamped on; modifications would have been needed. The air that Anderson had so conscientiously collected from far and near was practically exhausted, the evening was advancing, and they were all getting tired after six days of it. Impatient for success.

"All in all," M said, "the only road open to us is to try the plastic explosive. The cutter's done its bit. I know you've been dying to use it, Chief," Thistleton-Smith continued to Thorns. The Chief beamed. Like pure plasticine, it was, and Thorns was back in his childhood toying with it. Quickly he stuck his two-inch circle of the stuff on the rear door, inserted a detonator to fire it, and attached a fuse ready to light. M, Anderson, and Walden took cover in a near-by fold of the down. The Chief lit his fuse, glanced quickly at his watch, and scampered gaily back to the other three. "All right, Chief? How many more seconds have we got?" M asked.

"Just about fifteen now, sir, I make it. Twelve . . . ten . . . eight . . . six . . . four . . . two . . . one" . . . *Bang!*

The Chief's charge fired. A bird fluttered off. The mine was all right. Complete calm again. The sun had set. They waited, breathless. A few more seconds for luck.

"Should be all right now," M pronounced. "Come on, let's go and see." They had been sheltering about two hundred and fifty yards off. They all set out at a brisk walk. M hurried ahead of the rest a little. After about ninety seconds he was fifty yards off the mine. A sudden flash . . . a sharp, cracking burst . . . and M was flat on his face in the long grass. The others dropped within the second. M parted the blades, peeped up, and saw much of the mine in bits—and blazing. The heavy battery landed a yard in front of him. He put his head down again. Vicious bits of metal showered and scattered among—and beyond—the others. The parachute shackle landed on the lorry a hundred yards off. Then it was peace again. M looked back to the others. None of them was hurt. One by one they got up, brushed down, and moved in to put the flames out. Chief surveyed the scene sadly.

It was all too clear that the mechanically operated charge they were trying to get at inside the rear door had fired—after a delay. Why the time-lag no one knew.

"Good job we didn't break into a trot to get up to it," Anderson said, unusually soberly for him, "or we really would have run right into it! And it would have paid us out properly. Never have lived it down—if we *had* lived. The Chief lights a fuse. We all take cover. Count out the seconds. And then rush right into it!"

As it was, they reckoned themselves lucky to have got away with it without any injuries.

The remains of the mine resembled those at Boarhunt, although the mechanism seemed a little less damaged.

"Don't look glum, you two," M tried to cheer Anderson and Walden, who had grown somewhat attached to their mine after a 144-hour vigil with it. "It's just as well it has happened this way. That thing would have been the very devil to tackle, and even if you'd managed it the trial and tribulation just wouldn't have been worth it. I don't somehow think we'll hear of this sort of thing any more."

They looked their last on what was left of the black shell and crumpled metal. A hole had been ripped out of the rear door, and the mangled metal of the shell itself was folded back by the force of the eruption.

M clambered into his car with a headache and a sense of some elation and relief. There had been no more casualties, thank God.

As at Boarhunt, all the bits were faithfully gathered up and transported to *Vernon* for the boffins. Their findings confirmed the beliefs suggested by the first of the two mines. There had definitely been a triple booby-trap, arranged so that any attempt to remove the rear door would have operated one of two electrical switches, or a third mechanical switch! Again, no magnetic unit was found, nor could the mine reasonably have been laid in error ten miles inland, among the hills. The conclusion was inescapable. From the highest authority in the Reich the orders must have come: stop them stripping German mines. From Hitler himself, perhaps. But the plan—like the mines—misfired. The tragedy at *Vernon* had not been in vain.

"Gives you a queer feeling," M said to Ouvry later. "Up till now everything's been impersonal, even the *Vernon* affair. But this has been aimed at us individually. A personal present from the Fuehrer." Less discriminate directives were to fall in the following month. . . .

6

Land Mines on London

ONE more interlude occurred before Enemy Mining Section really returned to the sight and sound of sea. For within a month of the booby-trap episode the Germans launched on London their vicious land-mine war. Although the bomb-fuse had suggested the possibility of their use on land, no one really envisaged that mines would be brought to bear for such wholesale devastation of the capital—and, later, elsewhere. Fortunately for us quite a large percentage of them failed to explode on contact as intended, and an immediate and unexpected need arose for them to be rendered safe, solely to let life flow on in the stricken city. This was the difference between normal work and the fight against the land mines: *Vernon* was acting only for safety's sake, and not for what might lie inside the mines. Until an organization could be created to handle all those reported not exploded, then, *Vernon* stepped into the breach again.

Hodges was Duty Mining Officer on Monday night, September 16. At 0345 he got back to his office after an air-raid alarm, just in time to hear the phone ringing. It was the Flag Officer in Charge, London. "I thought I'd better let you know. Three parachute mines have been dropped on London. Two of them at Edmonton and one at Walthamstow."

LIEUTENANT-COMMANDER J. G. D. OUVRY, D.S.O., R.N.

EQUALLY TERRIBLE FROM
ALL ANGLES

Four views of the first German
magnetic mine to be recovered and
made safe—one of the most
hazardous and vital operations of
the whole War.

Photos H.M.S. "Vernon"

LOADING THE FIRST GERMAN MAGNETIC MINE FOR
CONVEYANCE TO PORTSMOUTH AFTER IT HAD BEEN
RENDERED SAFE
Photo H.M.S. "Vernon"

MINE ASHORE ON THE EAST COAST
Its primer and detonator out, it is now safe.
Photo Planet News

(*above*) EIGHT OFFICERS OF THE SERVICE MOST SILENT

Photographed in the grounds of H.M.S. *Vernon*.

(*left*) HIS MAJESTY KING GEORGE VI DECORATING COMMANDER OUVRY WITH THE D.S.O.

Lieutenant-Commander Lewis, who was also awarded the D.S.O., can be seen between His Majesty and Ouvry, while the C.-in-C., Portsmouth, Admiral Sir William James, is on the King's left.

LIEUTENANT-COMMANDER ROY EDWARDS INVESTIGATING A COMPONENT OF AN ENEMY MINE AND *(left)* EMPTYING HIS POCKETS OF ALL METALLIC OBJECTS WHICH MIGHT FIRE A MAGNETIC MINE

Commander Edwards was later killed on the East Coast while tackling a mine of this very kind.

Photos Planet News

(*above*) GERMAN MINE
ASHORE AT
LOWESTOFT IN 1942

Lieutenants Turner and
Mould on each side of a
Chief Petty Officer. The
civilian scientist in Home
Guard uniform is Mr
Walden, who was decorated
for his work in rendering
mines safe.

(*left*) LIEUTENANT-
COMMANDER
EDWARDS ON THE
EAST COAST IN UN-
PLEASANT COMPANY

OFFICERS AND WRENS OF H.M.S. "VERNON" MINING DEPARTMENT

The officer in charge was Commander (M), now Rear-Admiral G. Thistleton-Smith, G.M., R.N., seated in the centre of the second row. Commander Ouvry is next to him at the right.

HITLER'S SECRET WEAPON NUMBER ONE—THE MAGNETIC MINE

The mine is lying harmlessly on a *Vernon* trolley. Credit for its conquest goes to Commanders Ouvry and Lewis, Chief Petty Officer Baldwin (later killed), and Able Seaman Vearncombe.

Photo H.M.S. "Vernon"

SCAFFOLDING SUNK
TWENTY-SEVEN FEET DEEP
TO GET AT A MINE
DROPPED FROM THE AIR

The Army gives a helping hand
before *Vernon* officers tackle
the mine.

ONE OF THE FIRST
LAND MINES DROPPED
ON LONDON

The mine fell in a backyard in
Edmonton. *Vernon* officers
hurried up by car to tackle this
mine—and many others.

(*above*) A.R.P. WORKERS AT
CLACTON REMOVING A MAGNETIC
MINE FOR FURTHER INSPECTION

(*left*) FUSE FROM THE FIRST
MAGNETIC MINE

(*bottom, left*) A GERMAN
MAGNETIC MINE WITH PARA-
CHUTE STILL ATTACHED

(*bottom, right*) LAND MINE
WHICH FELL ON COVENTRY AND
FAILED TO EXPLODE

A FRIENDLY INSCRIPTION ON AN ALUMINIUM FLOAT WHICH KEEPS A MINE ON THE RIGHT SLEW

A free translation might read:
"If I guide you well and true,
    Churchill will be in the stew."

FIRST GERMAN MOORED ANTENNA MINE FOUND IN THE WAR

Most mines *Vernon* handled were non-contact—magnetic, acoustic, or pressure.

Photo H.M.S. "Vernon"

DESTINATION DOWNING STREET

German land mine bearing caricature of Mr Churchill, complete with cigar.

Photo H.M.S. "Vernon"

GERMAN BOMB MINE INTENDED FOR USE ON LAND OR IN THE WATER

To prevent its secrets being discovered it was fitted with a firing device which operated if the mine were laid in too shallow water. A = Access holes to fixing-bolts. B = Access holes to rear-cover fixing-bolts. C = Tail-fixing brackets and bolts.

DEVICE DEVELOPED TO CUT THROUGH SHELL OF ENEMY
MINE BY REMOTE CONTROL

Some one then had to get his hand inside the hole and
disconnect the various booby-traps and circuits.

AMERICAN NAVAL OFFICER BESIDE A MINE CAPTURED
AT BIZERTA

Photo H.M.S. "Vernon"

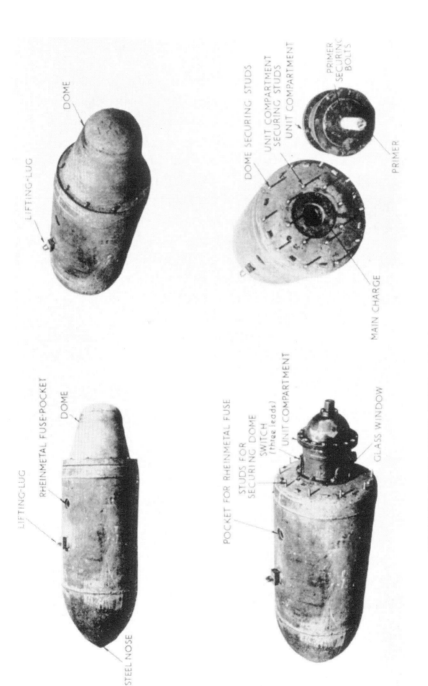

GERMAN BOMB MINE WITH ANTI-STRIPPING BOOBY-TRAP

If it were found unexploded and its dome removed, photo-electric cells behind a glass window (*lower left*) would operate the firing circuit.

ENEMY MINE ASHORE IN HEAVY SEAS AT HASTINGS

A lieutenant, *his cigarette still alight*, secures it to near-by coastal defences, and then retires to await low tide, when it can be handled with greater safety.

Photo Sport and General

MAKING LIGHT OF IT

An enemy mine being recovered for examination from a Malayan mangrove swamp.

REMOVING THE DETONATOR FROM A MINE WASHED UP ON THE SHORES OF THE NETHERLANDS EAST INDIES

GERMAN AIRCRAFT-LAID MINES ABANDONED NEAR BRUSSELS IN 1944

Personnel of H.M.S. *Vernon* saw that they were all safe—with the aid of the American forces.

"Right," checked Hodges, staggered and sleepy after an hour in a *Vernon* shelter. "I'll let Commander M know, and we'll come up in the morning."

"Thanks. Make it as early as you can, because we've had to evacuate a couple of thousand people from Edmonton alone."

By 0800 M, Hodges, and Anderson, with all the gear, were away. "Go up the Great West Road to London, will you, driver?" M asked. "I was told to keep an eye open along that particular route for some sort of escort."

Soon after Staines a full-scale police escort came slap up to them, wheeled round smartly, and overtook the grey naval car, then motioned it to a standstill. "Good morning, sir." The police officer greeted them with a salute. "We suggest you follow us at 40 m.p.h., and we'll whisk you through all the red lights if you're agreeable."

"Good Lord, no!" M exploded. "The speed's all right, but let's get there a few minutes later—and alive. We shan't be much good to you any other way, you know."

The policeman chuckled. "Very well, sir. Sorry I was a bit overeager. But it's pretty grim seeing all those people pushed out of their homes."

The cars and motor-cycles screeched to a stop near the site of the first mine. It was a normal type C, so M left Hodges to deal with it, going on to the second specimen with Anderson. Hodges' "horror" had fallen in a tiny backyard of one of a row of small semi-detached houses. It had smashed through the roof of an outhouse and buried its nose in the ground. By the smell it seemed that a drain had burst, too. It had come to rest just outside the back door. The wee kitchenette showed signs of a hasty exit—the table still laid for supper, a dish of tomatoes in place. The bomb-fuse was visible on top.

Hodges cleaned the grit from the fuse with a boot-brush. An easy-chair made an ideal nest to receive the fuse as it was extracted. Having got thus far, Hodges, acting on orders, awaited the return of the others.

M and Anderson polished off number two, which had dropped on a hard tennis-court in the middle of a recreation ground, and was entangled in its parachute. They returned to the scene of the first. Anderson, more experienced than Hodges, took over. "I think we'd better get the fuse out from as far away as possible." He rigged a line from the fuse, over a wall and out into the street through a narrow alley. The three stood stock-still while Anderson tugged sharply on the line. No bang. They clambered back into the kitchen. There lay the fuse, nestling on the easy-chair Hodges had so thoughtfully provided.

"Okay. You can come in and get it now," M called to the A.R.P. squad, who had been anxiously eyeing the proceedings throughout the afternoon, knowing that their own houses surrounded the site. A cheer broke out, and they piled in to dig it out and finally get it away on a trolley.

"How about the third?" M asked the police officer, who had stayed near them all day.

"Didn't I tell you? Some mad Irishman dashed in and dealt with it earlier this morning before you got up here. A miracle he wasn't blown sky-high, I should say."

"Well, that's one less for us, I suppose," said Anderson.

As the mine was loaded on to its lorry word got round that the *Vernon* trio were through. M congratulated the A.R.P. on their work, and received thanks in return. As they drove down the street surging crowds shouted, wept, thanks—voiced from deep down. For a day they had been homeless. Now they were going back in safety —the safety of September 1940.

"Well worth while," M said thoughtfully. The other two silently agreed. All three of them slept the whole way home, except for a snack at the Cricketer's Arms, Bagshot. The day ended at *Vernon* just after 2300.

Twenty-four hours later, before midnight on Tuesday, the phone went once more in the Duty Officer's room. Anderson answered it. "More mines on London," came the report. He dug out M, who arranged for Lieutenant Speirs and Hodges and Sub-Lieutenant Wadsley to accompany Anderson by car at 0800, just as on the previous day. At the Admiralty they found Ryan, the two-and-a-half ringer who had helped down at Clacton, and Commander Obbard. The *Vernon* trio (Speirs, Hodge, and Wadsley) worked without the safety horn that Diver Tawn used under water.

Speirs and Hodges paired off to go to Woolwich, where they found their mine already dealt with by Sub-Lieutenant Danckwerts, a former pupil of Hodges, when he was a schoolmaster. All they had to do was remove the clock. Anderson and Wadsley joined them, having found that they too had been beaten to their mine by Danckwerts.

"I think I'd better catch up with this chap," Anderson decided, "and warn him in case he kills himself in his hurry!"

Anderson left, and Wadsley told the other two how an old lady, watching the mine at Kidbrooke Park, insisted on seeing inside the mine, and brought her umbrella to

G

bear against the policeman who tried to intercept. "I've paid my rates and taxes, so I'm entitled to see what's going on in my borough," she had declared vociferously. Nothing or no one was going to stop her.

Speirs and Hodges rendered two safe during the rest of the day, and reported to the Admiralty next morning at 1030 for further orders. As they waited in an outer office Anderson and Wadsley walked in, subdued.

"Hello, you two!" Hodges said excitedly. "You look as if you've just been through the proverbial hedge. What happened?"

Neither of them was very communicative. They had come in to make their report. "If you really want to know," Anderson answered, "we ran into a bit of trouble."

"Actually there's a funny side to it." Wadsley smiled. The Sub had dark hair and a fresh complexion, his round cheeks savouring of the sea. "We were working near a building on a type D, and the fuse started to go. The gardens were damned difficult to negotiate. I hopped over a fence or two. Anderson was behind me. When I reckoned I'd got far enough I got my head down quick. None too soon really, for the thing blew up a couple of seconds later. When it was all over I got up and trotted back a bit, looking for Anderson. I couldn't see him anywhere. Then from the far corner of the garden something stirred! There was an unearthly rattle of old corrugated iron, and then part of a compost-heap got up and walked towards me! Anderson really put his foot in it this time! Actually it was pretty bad. He was only thirty yards off when it fired—too close for comfort."

They all enjoyed this anecdote, but were duly sympathetic with the boss. The uncertainty of it all stayed uppermost in their minds. They did not want to sit still and think too much just then. The best thing was to be up and doing.

Speirs and Hodges were sent down to Hammersmith soon after Wadsley had finished recounting his tale, with C.P.O. Godwin. One in the morning there, and then on to Barnes. A type D lay on the railway bridge near Clifford Avenue. All the houses near were already evacuated for a radius of a thousand yards. The bomb-fuse was underneath the mine. Speirs moved round and extracted the detonator. Hodges stuffed the parachute round the mine to stop it rolling down on them. Then he tackled the ring of the clock. It was stiff. He tapped it round with a punch. The fuse started whizzing . . . they ran for it. Speirs got twice as far as Hodges. He touched down at seventy-five yards. Hodges slipped, lay thirty-five yards off, counted the last few seconds, prayed, prayed. . . .

The full fury roared towards him—only a hundred feet off. Hot blast shook him to the roots, bruised him. His ears discharged. But he was all right. Speirs dashed back, propped him up. "Don't worry, old man. I'll get a call through. Won't take a minute. Just keep still."

"Thanks," whispered Hodges.

Speirs rushed down on to the road, into the first house with a phone-wire showing. He got through to Richmond Hospital. In no time an ambulance was there. "Give me the Admiralty, please," Speirs asked the operator immediately after. He got his report in; Hodges was picked up; Speirs went on to Willesden to the next mine.

Hodges recovered quite quickly. Two weeks later he learned that Ryan and one or two others with him had been killed, including Chief Petty Officer Ellingworth. Hodges had tackled his first mine with the Chief. Rough luck.

Meanwhile Anderson had been assigned to Luton, where part of a factory was incapacitated by a non-exploded land mine. He left Town at mid-morning, reaching the factory about noon. The immediate vicinity was cleared, Anderson rendered the thing safe, and the Mayor took his hand warmly in congratulation. The girls of the factory chorused their approval.

"Of course," whispered the Mayor, "I know they've fallen for you in that uniform, but I'll let you into a secret. They're cheering for something else too. The little building next to the mine was the main ladies lavatory in the works, and it's been strictly out of bounds since first thing this morning! You can tell how long that's been!"

Anderson thanked them all, waved good-bye, and called out from the running-board of the car, "Sorry if I've inconvenienced you ladies. If some one had told me on the phone I'd have made the effort and been here earlier in the day."

For their courageous work the London pioneers were honoured by the King. Danckwerts received the George Cross; Hodges, Wadsley, Speirs, and Obbard the George Medal.

The days that followed were of never-ending activity. Many volunteers came forward from H.M.S. *King Alfred*, the officers' training establishment at Hove. Ouvry, now with Anderson as his assistant, instructed them, arranged to tool them up, sent them off to the front line. Tragedies there were inevitably, but remarkably and thankfully few. Lessons were learned. New ideas and new tools followed. Gradually a separate organization was set up at the Admiralty of officers and ratings. Captain C. N. E. Currey was called in to take charge, and *Vernon* eventually relieved of the responsibility of dealing with mines of known types which had not been covered by water.

The pioneers stepped out. Others moved in. Still in London, Lieutenant Gidden reported for duty to the Admiralty one morning soon afterwards. "There's a mine on the main Charing Cross railway-line right in the middle of Hungerford Bridge, sir," the duty rating told him. Gidden did not wait to hear more. The car shot down Northumberland Avenue, where ten months earlier Ouvry had snatched an hour's sleep before his trip to Shoeburyness. The car swung on to the Embankment, ground to a halt. A peak-capped police officer saluted. "It's worse than we thought at first, Lieutenant. Before the railway people had time to switch off the juice it fused itself to the conductor rail. I'll come up and show you."

Row upon row of green carriages were lined up in the station. The bridge was at a standstill. Big Ben glistened in the autumn sunshine. Waterloo Bridge stood proud and white. St Paul's, too, unbowed. The breeze blew fresh on the bridge.

"That's all right now, thanks, officer. I can see it now. I'll signal to you as soon as it's all clear, but don't go letting them switch the current on till I say. I don't want a few thousand volts through me."

Alone, with the sweep of the Thames underfoot, and the rusted framework of Hungerford. And the mine lying squarely across the live line. "Live line," that's what the Southern used to call it before the War. Never thought I'd see one this close, though. Gidden got out his hammer and chisel. There was no other way. He could not render it till it was clear of the line. A slight tap. He listened acutely. No whirr. A little harder. Still quiet. It was hard to hear in the wind. Must be careful. No sense in getting myself killed just because I'm not listening. Another tap. And another. A hit. Two. Three. Slowly it moved. The breeze tore through the bridge. The wait was over. The mine came clear. In the course of his career Gidden was awarded the G.C., G.M., and O.B.E.

The land-mine menace spread north. To Coventry, Glasgow, Liverpool. And on Merseyside one landed in a gasholder, suspended only by the supports of the construction. The gas-holder was lowered as far as it would go. Lieutenant Harold Newgass climbed out on to the supports. The mine wavered in the wind. Newgass steadied and secured it, rendered it safe, clambered back. For this he was awarded the George Cross.

One Saturday night a land mine landed on the outskirts of a small Midlands country town. Two officers arrived on the scene during Sunday afternoon.

"This one's all yours, Kelly, old boy," said Miller, who had been sent up with the young two-ringer about to be 'blooded.' "But don't worry, now," the senior added. "If there's anything in the world you want, just say the word, and I'll come running—even out of the trench. That reminds me. We'll have to get cracking if we're going to get this done in daylight, so come on and see what help we can muster in the trench warfare."

The local police had evacuated the few houses and cottages in the immediate area. Willing helpers dug a slit trench for the Navy men who were so far from the sea—nearly in the very heart of England, in fact. Quite an anachronism. "Join the Navy and see the Midlands." So said Miller to ease any tension Kelly might be feeling. Miller remembered his own first time. It was no joke, however much you gritted your teeth. Things got you on edge.

By teatime everything was ready.

"Sure you're O.K.?"

"I'm fine—thanks."

Kelly emerged from the slit trench, walked over to the mine, adjusted his field-phone back to Miller, and reported all correct. The trench was strategically situated so that if the fuse started its familiar theme on one note the comparative safety of the trench could be reached before the twenty-three seconds ticked off. Always assuming that part of the time had not run on the clock's contact with the ground.

Kelly began operations. In his mind he had a clear picture of the processes. Must keep alert. He repeated the sequence as he prepared for his initiation. Chalking number one up can be the devil, he had overheard some ass saying back at Admiralty. But he was right, unfortunately.

Kelly applied himself to the task, but became aware that his mind was wandering. What the hell? Mustn't lose my grip. What's worrying me? He paused, pondered.

Then it struck him. He could hear music. Distantly, but distinctly. Only when he listened acutely did it sound loud in his ears, but all the time it was there. An unmistakably steady stream of hymns! The Salvation Army had taken up their accustomed stance in the square, and were well into the third tune. Kelly stood there bemused for a moment. He knew something had been putting him out of his stride. More; he was damned if he did not know this third hymn. What was it? He had stopped work altogether now to rack his brain. He knew it, or had done at school. That's it. Got it. "Nearer, my God, to Thee!" Of all the blessed cheerful things to choose, that takes the cake! Suddenly he burst out laughing, and spoke over the phone to Miller.

"I say, sir, I can't do a damned thing with that band. It's getting on my nerves. Do you think you could possibly get them to stop for a while. I shan't be long. Then they can play to their heart's—and soul's—content."

"I know just how it must be. It was beginning to irritate me too."

Miller was gone only a matter of minutes. He explained to the leader of the band that Kelly was dealing with a tricky mine, and needed all his wits about him. The Salvationist understood at once.

Kelly stood his ground in the quiet sunset spell. The distant hills darkened.

"Okay, now, Kelly." The voice brought him back with a jerk.

He went to work with a will. No nerves interrupted the sequence. Half-way now. Round the bend and into the home stretch. As he started on the last operation but one it happened. Whirr went the fuse. Anything from three to twenty-three seconds.

Kelly dropped everything and ran. The trench looked a long way off. He could 'get there in about fifteen flat. Six, seven, eight, nine, ten—an eruption of earth. It had gone off. Kelly was not caught by the explosion, but the blast lifted him bodily and swept him yards away into the middle of a bunch of bushes, leaving him stunned but unhurt.

Miller ran forward. The police constable and a Home Guard followed. Between them they carried Kelly into the nearest inhabited cottage. In the quiet of the living-room he came round mistily. He blinked. His brain cleared. He heard the clock ticking on the mantelpiece.

"What happened?"

"Keep still a bit, old chap. You got a free lift, but it looks as if no bones are broken."

The door-bell sounded sharply. It opened straight into the room, as is the arrangement in old country cottages. Kelly did not turn, but the others saw the red-and-black uniform of the Salvation Army.

"He'll be all right?" the newcomer whispered. "He must be all right. As soon as we heard he was tackling that mine we went right down on our knees in the market-place and prayed that nothing should happen to him— so he's got to be all right."

"Well, you've been answered," admitted Miller, "and mighty grateful we are for your thoughts." Then, after a pause: "But, you know, I reckon anyone would have got fed up with that particular tune at that particular moment!"

Back in London, the blitz went on. Edward Woolley, Lieutenant, sat in the Admiralty at 1745 one afternoon in October. "Oh, Woolley," called Captain Currey, "come in a second, will you? There's a tricky one for you near the Thames. Here are the whereabouts. Some wharf or other down by the docks. Not much more I can tell you about it. You know enough by now, anyway, to be telling me the job. Good luck, Woolley."

Little did Currey know that Woolley was to need it.

The Lieutenant reached the spot, in company with Able Seaman Pearson. An A.R.P. officer pointed up to the third storey of a flour-store. "That's where it dropped, sir, and there's been not a murmur from it since."

"Thanks. We'll shin up somehow and have a look at it."

The whole store and surrounding buildings were evacuated. Bags of flour lay piled high on all sides. But no sound. In the half-light Woolley shivered involuntarily. They were alone. And it was chilly, eerie. They groped their way to the third floor, looked round, saw only more sacks. Then right at the end the sky showed through a ragged hole in the roof. Carrying his gaze downward, Woolley saw the mine, dark against the fawn of the sacks. He looked more closely. Still the light was poor. He could not do the job in the gloom. Windows were conspicuous only by their absence. Then he saw the doors overlooking the river. He moved carefully round the mine. Neither of them spoke. The ancient floorboards sagged with each step. A rat ran across his path. Softly Woolley undid the latch, pushed the doors wide, and the cool evening air floated in. Plus a little light. Through these doors the sacks were lowered at high tide into barges below. But now it was low water. No barges lingered there. All he saw fifty feet below was the slimy mud of the river-bed, glistening in the sunset.

He turned his back on the scene, strode over to the mine, tapped the securing-ring slightly to try to unscrew it—and the bomb-fuse started to run. So did they.

Panic for a second. No way out through the store. It would all come down on them. Twenty-three seconds to live—or less. It may have already run off part. They rushed over to the only outlet—the doors on to the river. Woolley stripped off his coat, looked down. Cold, oozing mud glowered at him. He turned, ten yards from the mine . . . paused . . . stood . . . each leg pulling in a different direction. The clockwork stopped ticking. Everything inside him stopped for a second with it.

"Thank God," he breathed to Pearson.

All was peace again. A gull hovered by the flapping doors, then wheeled off.

They went back to the mine. Woolley tapped the ring again. It gave a little. Then the tell-tale whirr. A second time they tore over to the doors, quicker this time. They leant over to plunge . . . stopped. Woolley glanced up at Pearson. The sailor shook his head. No. Not that. Anything rather than that awful mess below. Both their brains pounded. Seconds passed. Then the whirr stopped again. The mechanism jammed, as it had done before. A technical hitch. The decision was made for them. They returned to the mine. Next time it was all right. No more whirring. No more decisions. It was safe—and so were they.

7

Acoustic Attack

BACK in the spring of 1940 the Germans realized that we had mastered the magnetic mine. So the High Command ordered their technical experts to develop an acoustic unit at the highest possible priority. This was to be a complete change. The first German acoustic mines went into production in July, and by the end of August it duly became apparent to Britain that some such weapon was now being laid. Enemy mines were firing at widely varying distances from ships. A destroyer sailing at speed through a certain channel set off a mine far farther afield than a smaller and slower vessel had done a little while earlier. Both ships had been degaussed against magnetic mines. Neither had come in direct contact with mines. Something fresh was afoot. It seemed likely that the faster destroyer, with its more penetrative sound-pressure, had actuated an acoustic unit of some kind or another. But it was not known at what frequency in cycles the mine would respond, so until an actual specimen was recovered intact—as at Shoeburyness the previous November in the case of the magnetic mine— no definite sweeping operations could be devised by way of combat.

The facts, as subsequently revealed, were that the booby-trap efforts at North Boarhunt and Piddlehinton of August 16 had been timed to a nicety by the precise minds of the High Command. The Germans probably reckoned that for a long, long time afterwards no one would go near a mine if it were dropped in error on a beach or in shallow water. They thought that they were safe to launch the second secret weapon of the War— the acoustic mine. Accordingly, on August 28, the first batch of these was dropped. As before, the Admiralty could only prepare for the time when they would be able to recover one. Casualties began to occur.

Meanwhile Enemy Mining Section were fully occupied by the land mines. The need to get hold of an acoustic mine flowed as a dramatic undercurrent through the early stages of the battle of London. August passed. The War was one year old. A flourishing infant that looked like growing for some time before it died. October. For two months acoustics were laid in the channels surrounding our shores. German pilots had been briefed to take special precautions when laying them. Flying overland was strictly *verboten*. Mines were to be laid only to catch targets well clear of the coast.

Now it was autumn. Mine Design Department moved out of *Vernon*. First to the Portsmouth Grammar School, with its leisurely labyrinth of chemistry labs and classrooms. Next to Commercial Chambers, a tall, glassy office block hardly suitable as a refuge from the Luftwaffe. Then out of the city altogether, to the idyllic country-side between Havant and Rowlands Castle. Commander M and the naval side went too, later, leaving as few as possible at Portsmouth. *Vernon* was bombed badly, but not before practically all important branches had been safely evacuated.

Thistleton-Smith, Ouvry, and the rest first saw West

Leigh Cottage on a golden morning in October. They motored through a dormant Havant, turning northward. At the crossroads a mile out of the town the car swung right down a lane lined with beech-trees shedding their leaves through the blue-smoky air. Fluttering down into the ditches, leaving just the solemn spikes of the branches. Past West Leigh House, a square, greystone building with a terrace away to the south, an ornamental pond on the west, and stables where guests' horses once got back their breath on just such an autumn morning many years before. Stables which were to become a fitting-shop. A winding drive from the House inside the grounds led down to the Cottage. M's department moved into the Cottage; trials and scientific sections into the House; and the main Design Department found a fresh and more peaceful home at Leigh Park House. Here, through the conservatory and on to the terrace, a steep lawn sloped dramatically down to a large lake, nestling far from the wind and embraced by a flaming autumn cluster of chestnuts. No breeze shimmered over its waters. Only the lilies lay across the mirror-like surface. The water was still. Mines were being devised to destroy. Yet the water was still. Not so, near the mouth of the river Ogmore, by Porthcawl, on the night of Sunday, October 27; the streaming seas of the North Atlantic whipped into the Welsh shore. A squadron of enemy planes veered unsteadily overhead in the black, buffeted above a foreign coast. Suddenly the familiar dark cylinder dropped clear of an undercarriage; a parachute stopped it short in its plummet seaward, and a soft splash in the night announced that it had fallen fair and square into thirty feet of water, which dried out at low tide. Either the Germans never realized just how far the tide recedes round the British Isles, or their pilots overshot the mark more than once.

As soon as it was seen, when the water fell clear the following forenoon, Flag Officer in Charge, Cardiff, reported its presence to *Vernon,* adding that the proposal was to try to explode it. *Vernon* signalled back urgently: "Save it at all costs. D.T.M. [Director of Torpedoes and Mining] are sending some one down to look at it." Coincidentally, Lieutenant-Commander Chapple, D.S.C., R.N.V.R., was on leave in Cardiff, and went over to investigate first. As a result, Lieutenant S. Baker, R.N.V.R., and Sub-Lieutenant P. A. Cummins, R.N.V.R., arrived on the scene. *Vernon* personnel were still busy with the land mines. Cummins went into the attack. He knew that it might be an acoustic. One tap at an unknown frequency, high-pitched or low, might write finis to the mine—and the man.

Soon after 2300 on Monday night, October 28, Cummins set out. The night was cold, the South Wales coast cheerless. The mine lay 400 yards below high-water and 100 yards above low-water mark. Between the two, in other words. It rested rather diffidently in a shallow depression in the sand. Cummins picked it out with his torch. The wind ricocheted across the watery sand. He wished he had worn a high-neck sweater. It was a lonely vigil. His single wavy stripe on each arm echoed the loneliness. The gold gleamed dully in the torchlight. A young man on a strange shore. Alone with a strange shape. Only a year in the Navy. Cummins shone the torch on the shell. It seemed a standard type C. The characters Ld 335 were stencilled on it, dimly discernible. The safety-ring of the primer release was still in place.

But the forked pin itself was missing. The primer release had not operated, so he groped in his jacket for a short stub of lead pencil, let it slip through his icy fingers to the sand, retrieved it dampened, and pushed it through the ring, to make sure the pin stayed in place overnight, while another tide washed over it. Cummins then drove a stake into the soft sand, and attached the mine to it, in case it should try to escape before daylight. He retraced his footmarks over the bed of the estuary, back to Porthcawl. Scant signs he saw of his outward tread. The imprints had all but been swallowed up by the fluid, plastic sands. So far so good, he thought. Then a line from one of the Laurel and Hardy comedies flashed through his brain as he reached the shingle. "So far so good," proclaimed Hardy to Stan. Came the classic response: "Not very far, Olly!" Cummins felt like Stan Laurel just then. He smiled. The taut half-hour he had spent suddenly snapped. He uncoiled. "Not very far," he muttered to himself, remembering the blank, bland face of Laurel gazing into his partner's full moon.

No moon for him that night, though. Nor sun next morning.

Low water fell about 1100. At 1030 Baker and Cummins trudged out after the ebbing tide. They took out the primer, which had somehow not released. The detonator was found to have fired. To the clock six leads were found. Behind it a nine-volt battery. The standard procedure was complete. The mine was adjudged safe. It was got aboard a lorry and dispatched forthwith to *Vernon*.

"All too easy, Baker," was Cummins' only comment. "I only hope it's as straightforward as it seems. I

can't think why the primer didn't release and the thing
go off before we ever got to it. I suppose it *was* a
magnetic."

In fact, it was the first acoustic to be recovered.

"What are we going to call the mine investigation
range?" M asked Anderson, whom he intended to set in
charge of the special party there.

"I don't really know, sir. Seems rather a mouthful,
doesn't it, at the moment? And it's got to be a code
name to cover its identity. M for Mine . . . I for Investigation . . . R for Range. M.I.R." Anderson repeated the
letters slowly, deliberately. "We don't want it to sound
too grim. A girl's name would be the sort of thing, I
suppose, to cloak its purpose. Mir. Why, of course.
Mirtle! H.M.S. *Mirtle*."

Thus the range became known. To this day its location
stays secret.

The mine was sent on from *Vernon* to *Mirtle*, set in a
remote chalk escarpment, to be treated on the 31st.

Walden accompanied the dockyard driver (one of the
many who risked their lives transporting live mines about
the country for *Vernon*) in the lorry carrying the mine to
Mirtle.

Not far from their destination, on a very steep hill,
the driver missed his gears when changing down to negotiate the gradient with his heavy burden. With the
sudden change, the vehicle shot forward—and the mine
broke away from its lashings, crashed through the tail-
board, and smashed a way down four feet on to a rough
flintstone-encrusted road with a one-in-four-slope.

It careered downhill, and finally came to rest two
hundred yards away. Somehow or other Walden, the

H

driver, and a couple of ratings retrieved the mine and got it back aboard the lorry.

Relating the experience later to Anderson, Walden observed, "If ever a mine should have gone off—it was down that hillside!"

On the 31st, too, the six-lead clock, the bomb-fuse, and the primer release extracted at Porthcawl arrived at *Mirtle*. Examination of the primer showed that it had not been released owing to distortion of the top of the spindle. Otherwise, the whole thing would have gone off. The first impressions, together with the examination of the clock, suggested that the mine was a new type. Torrential rain hampered the work on October 31, but it cleared by Friday, November 1.

Anderson emerged from a caravan they used for work. Walden was with him, as he had been at Piddlehinton.

"Not going to take any chances this time, Walden, old boy," Anderson vouchsafed. "We'll stay here till we've rigged up as foolproof a way of unbuckling this thing as can be. I've a shrewd idea that we're going to find that the gear in the unit compartment will be different from anything we've seen before."

"I tell you what, Anderson. I would say for sure that there is another auxiliary charge similar to the *Vernon* mine. It seems that they still mean to stop us stripping it—for some reason or other."

"Anything else?"

"Yes. I think there might well be a clockwork mechanism. Have to be careful of that." Then, in a rather more excited voice, as if he had only just appreciated the significance of what he had said: "Damned careful!"

"But at least there was no ticking when we listened

yesterday with the headphones, was there?" Anderson asked.

"No, but we'd better try again now. Let's get alongside the pocket of the main clock," Walden suggested. "Should be about here. Now, dead quiet."

The rain had stopped. Only the wind whistled faintly over the hills. *Mirtle* lay inland. A sailor started to sing *Begin the Béguine* on the other side of the caravan.

"Stop that singing a minute," Anderson called. "We're listening for some ticking."

Again only the wind. Then Walden cried out excitedly, "Can you hear that? Very high-pitched. But quite distinct. If it's ticking we're closer than we should be."

"My God, I think you're right!" agreed Anderson. "Yes . . . you . . . are," he added slowly, listening between each word, so as not to miss a murmur. "An irregular, high-pitched click."

"That's it," Walden said, with the eager enthusiasm of the scientist on the verge of a discovery. "Very faint, but no doubt about it—not a shadow." Then, in a cautioning tone: "Right. Let's stop a minute and take stock. We won't do the slightest good by rushing things."

They walked over to the caravan which served as an office. "This is the position as I see it," the Lieutenant said. "Stop me if you don't agree. The clock mechanism, we know, can be set for any period up to six days. It can be adjusted to make the mine either passive or active after that time—or to explode it on the spot when the clockwork has run down. Now that the main detonator has fired, and as far as we know or can guess there's no other primer in the main explosive charge, if anything blows up it will be an auxiliary charge."

"I'm with you so far."

"Right. Now, the mine was laid on the night of Sunday the 27th to Monday the 28th. If this clock mechanism we've found has the same setting as we've met previously, and is used here to fire an auxiliary charge, then the unit will be destroyed some time before the night of Saturday, November the 2nd to Sunday the 3rd. In other words, we've only got a day or two to strip it and find out if it's an acoustic—or what it is. Take back what I said about there not being any hurry! And there's the other little point, of course: that blessed clock's liable to stop any second. You know what that means if we're both mucking about here!"

Walden had already realized this. "I suppose you'll get in touch with M?"

"I'll ring him right now."

Anderson put the facts to the Commander, who was getting used to rapid action by this time—and even thriving on it. "Number One and I will come up first thing in the morning, Anderson. You can't do anything to-night in the dark. Just get a good rest."

The First Lieutenant had recovered from August the 6th. Nearly three months had passed since that black Tuesday. Now he was on his way to *Mirtle* with M to tackle the unknown all over again. More was known this time at least. They had a shrewd idea that the booby-trap was there. They would not walk into it, as poor P.O. Fletcher had done. Every minute counted now. They had Hitler's secret weapon number two in their hands, with the expectation of only twenty-four hours' life for it before it was liable to go off. Time was everything. And to stress it the clock went on ticking and clicking.

"It's certainly still going," declared M, bent double over the mine-shell, with his left ear frozen stiff against the metal, "but it's not a normal ticking, is it? Well, here we go again, chaps. Let's bring out the disc-cutter and try and get at the booby-trap—and find out where that blasted ticking's coming from."

The trap had to be dealt with before the rear door could be taken off and the secrets revealed.

The Piddlehinton process began all over again. Number One, Anderson, and Walden clamped on the trepanner, got out of range, and cut a four-inch-diameter hole out of the shell over the auxiliary charge. Walden took the smallest-size glove—6½—so got his hand in here and managed to swivel his wrist round till his fingers closed on the detonator to the auxiliary charge. With as tight a grip as he could muster, he clenched his hand round, and removed it cautiously, tensely. Each finger bit into the metal. He shut his teeth tight. Out it came.

"That's one stage," Anderson breathed in relief. "Listen. You can hear the clock more distinctly now through the hole." They cut a second hole where they hoped a battery might be—a battery which turned out to be mounted in the rim of the unit's frame. Walden had another go. The hole was well placed. The leads to the battery showed clearly as he peered into the neat little circle cut from the shell. His hands were tight, but he got them in. Rain was falling now. "Careful not to let any liquid on to the leads," warned Number One.

Walden successfully severed the leads. "Second stage over," he announced. "Now for the next one."

Before hole number three was cut over the clock they

glimpsed its mechanism through the second circle. This third hole had to be in the rear door of the mine, the upright fitment at the end whose removal had caused the *Vernon* disaster. The place settled for the hole was between the fins on the door. Special adaptors had already been made to support the cutting-machine in this upright position. The party trailed away. Then the familiar whirr of the cutter. The disc came out. And two additional batteries came to light inside, one of which consisted of two small torch batteries. They disconnected all the leads.

1800, Saturday, November 2. It was dark. Rain had fallen relentlessly all day. They were all drenched. "Come on; let's call it a day," Number One suggested. "Perhaps the sun will shine for us to-morrow. We can't do any more in this pitch blackness."

"Agreed." Anderson and Walden joined him in a race to the caravan.

The clock went on ticking into the night. But they felt that they must have cut any circuit it might make when it stopped.

Sunday morning, November 3. The weather had improved a little, but rain still fell spasmodically. Down at R.N. Barracks, Divisions were being held, and the morning service was running its predestined course. One or two matelots were looking at their watches as they calculated the time of the 'liberty boat' ashore from the barracks. The hands of the watches moved round. 1000 . . . 1015 . . . 1032. . . .

And the clock still ticked. "One more cut," Anderson proposed. "We ought to find any evidence of a mechanically operated destructive device—if there is one. We've cut the two electrical traps."

Back they trooped to the hideout.

"Don't you notice anything?" Number One shouted with glee. "The clock's stopped." And so it had. Their calculations were correct. A six-day clock. They had beaten it—and were alive.

The rain came down. The grass on the hills seemed deeper green. The mine-shell glistened as the rain poured on to it, streaming round the circumference and into the chalky grass beneath. And it rolled down the men's oil-skins, soaked their faces, dropped off their noses, blurred their eyes.

So to the final operation. The rear door could come off. But they were not going to get caught. A special contraption was rigged up to hold the door firm while the nuts were unscrewed one by one. The last spiralled off on to the sodden ground. Once more from a safe distance, they crouched down expectantly. Number One jerked a lever, and the door was wrenched free, dragging its rubber jointing-ring with it. Peace. No bang. It was all over. All over. The clouds burst over the hill towering above them. Sheets of water fell across the range. The whole mechanism was withdrawn from the compartment, got into a lorry, and sent to Mine Design Department. Accompanied by the inevitable question: "What is it?"

The mechanism was all mounted on a disc fitting in the fore end of the compartment—with the exception of a microphone mounted on a bar welded across the dome to the rear door of the mine. This was the clue. M.D.D. pounced on it to produce the solution—an acoustic mine, actuated from the sea-bed by the sound of ships' engines pulsing through the water.

.　　　　　.　　　　　.

"This is second in importance only to your magnetic mine," M told Ouvry when he saw him at West Leigh. "Now they can really get on and devise a sweep. It could have developed into a situation as serious as last November. Let's pray we never have to face anything like that again. Somehow I don't think we shall now."

Soon after this British minesweepers were being fitted with Kango vibrating hammers in watertight containers under the keel of the vessels. These made enough noise —at the right pitch—to detonate acoustic mines at safe distances. But the mines responded only at a certain sensitive pitch, so it was not until the microphone had been analysed from the Porthcawl specimen that the antidote could be introduced. Later the Germans switched to combined acoustic-magnetic circuits, and thereafter the mine war resolved itself into an ever more intricate battle of wits between mine-designers of both countries on the one hand and designers of sweeps on the other. As the acoustic mine was mastered and 1940 gave way to 1941 the turning-point was reached. Britain began to take the offensive. Our own acoustic mines appeared on the scene. But Enemy Mining Section still found full employment. Already Ouvry and his officers had handled several dozen German mines, apart from the large numbers on London and the provinces. Winter passed. The arrival of the three Australians coincided with the Germans' latest fling. But the Aussies were equal to it.

8

Daylight is Death

BLOSSOM was on the boughs of the cherry- and almond-trees as three figures from Down Under, still bronzed from the previous summer's sunshine of Sydney, jumped out of the car at West Leigh Cottage—Stuart Mould, of New South Wales, Hugh Syme, of Victoria, and Leon Goldsworthy, of Western Australia.

Commander M extended his hand. "I hear you've been doing some sterling work up in Town on these abominable land mines. And now we're glad to get you down here to give us a bit of a boost. In fact, you couldn't have come at a more opportune time, chaps."

"This sounds interesting, sir." Mould rubbed his hands to signify an itch for action. "What's brewing? I hope it's something a bit stronger than that weak tea we've had tossed at us from all sides since we got over here! The Aussies love tea—but not the railway-buffet kind."

"I think I can guarantee you that," smiled M. "If you really want to get cracking I suggest we all go in and see Lieutenant-Commander Ouvry, who's responsible for the section. We've just had reports of a new type of bomb mine that the Hun is dropping, and if it's used extensively we may need you three sooner than you expect. Ouvry will explain the technicalities to you, so that you're all ready on the top line."

In his office Ouvry was introduced to the Aussies, who clustered in a triangle round him. "If you don't mind carrying on, Ouvry, I'll get back to the grind. Trials of our own mines are taking more and more of our time nowadays—thank goodness. It's a sign that we're on the move at last. Best of luck to you three, anyway."

They all saluted, and M was gone—to continue his tireless round. "If you're all comfortable, chaps, I'll put the position of this new offering that Fritz has cooked up for us. It's a bomb mine, as Commander M has probably told you. The idea is that it can be used either as bomb or mine. There are several differences from previous efforts, though. It's dropped minus a parachute, with a drogue, or just an eggshell-blue cardboard tail. The High Command realize they've been drifting too far inland with 'chutes. It's designed to detonate instantaneously on impact with a hard surface, to fire with a ninety-second delay if it's dropped by mistake in shallow water less than twenty-four feet deep, but if it's dropped in a depth of water greater than four fathoms it becomes active as a mine."

"Quite ingenious," murmured Mould.

"That's not all," went on Ouvry. "As you perceive, the idea is partly to use the same design for two purposes, but also it's devised to stop us stripping one to find out how the circuit is arranged—and they're changing all the time, as, of course, you know. You see the point —instantaneous on land, after a short delay in shallow water, and live in deeper water. The secret-service boys warned us of these, but, as usual, it's up to us to try and strip them, as otherwise we can't sweep the things at sea."

"How about booby-traps?" Syme chipped in. "If a mine fails to go off as it should, can you cope with stripping it, then?"

"That's just what I was coming to," Ouvry continued. "On May the 10th, three days ago only, one of them did misfire in a raid on Glasgow. It actually dropped in a ploughed field in Dumbartonshire. Only the tail was showing, but it was enough to indicate that here was one of the new types. *Vernon* was notified. Wadsley, together with a Commander Ashe Lincoln and Lieutenant-Commander Fenwick—both Wavy Navy chaps—went up and confirmed it. I'll call Wadsley[1] in presently, and let him tell you the full story. But this is the crux of it all. We've reason to suspect a strange set-up. The mine was badly knocked about, and they went ahead with the latest drill we've adopted. The mine was deep down in the field, so they had it dug out by a working-party using non-magnetic spades. But, as they didn't really know what was within, they also had to be careful about noise—in case of an acoustic arrangement. So they put into practice a special procedure we're trying out. The gist of it is to make all your sounds at a pitch higher than a microphone inside would pick them up. A ship's frequency is pretty low, something around 250 cycles, and the microphone won't respond much to high-pitched noises. So that's what they did. The job of loosening the nuts of the rear casing, or dome, was managed by this technique, making sure to keep the

---

[1] Wadsley and Fenwick were the first people to discover that certain German midget submarines not only fired a torpedo, but also laid a magnetic mine.

dome on in case of booby-traps. Then it was removed from a safe distance. Fortunately for us none of the mechanism was working—due to the crack it had on impact. Scottish soil must be harder than the Germans imagined! Anyway, here comes the climax: inside they found the booby-trap to end all traps—photo-electric cells fitted behind little glass windows and connected to the main explosive circuit, so that the moment the dome was taken off the daylight should have operated the photo-electric cells and fired the whole works."

"My God!" Syme said, open-mouthed. "They're thorough, the Nazis. That's one we might not have thought of, eh?"

"It was certainly lucky that the thing was damaged enough not to work, yet not destroyed," Ouvry concluded. "Now they've tried just about everything. Magnetic. Acoustic. The booby-traps we're all familiar with. And photo-electric cells to stop us seeing inside. So this is the drill, chaps, for the bomb mine. If any of you have to tackle one that's not already smashed to smithereens you *must* do it after dark. We've reconstructed the selenium cells here, and a pale-blue light seems safe enough. That will be enough for you to work with. But, whatever you do, don't let in the light, or it'll mean a long spell of darkness for you! Don't think I'm trying to frighten you, but I must instil these things into your minds. I'm responsible, and I don't want any of you on my conscience for the rest of my life!"

Forty-eight hours later Mould got his first chance, at Milford Haven. The main charge had exploded, but the unit was thrown clear, so it was fairly plain sailing. Another seventy-two hours, and he was at Belfast, chasing one seven feet down in the ground. Next day at Stepney he met Syme, and together they tackled a third. Three in four days. All was still well. Another seventy-two hours, and Syme had his second call.

1241, May 22, 1941. Syme was back at West Leigh. "I'm going down to get some lunch, Leon," he announced to Goldsworthy. But he never got the meal, for the phone rang briskly and businesslike from inside the black Bakelite case. "At least we know what's inside that contraption—relays and a bell and no high explosive. I'll get it."

"Oh, Syme, it's Ouvry. Pop along to the office, will you? There's another of these magnetics by the look of it down in Wales. Mould's not available, so you'll be able to cope, won't you?"

"Sure, sir. I'll be with you in five seconds flat." And he was.

It was dusk when Syme reached Pembroke Dock. In a balloon-barrage field near by the R.A.F. kept a respectful watch on his mine. 1500 pounds of explosive slumbered sullenly slightly below ground-level. The biggest bombs yet used in the War. Nearly three-quarters of a ton of the stuff. Enough to shake the whole station.

"I'll be glad of a working-party in the morning," Syme told the Station Commander, after examining the thing. "I've brought some non-magnetic spades and other gear we'll want. Shall we say 0930 in the morning, then, and I hope by dark we'll have it exposed enough for me to tackle the mechanism without risk of getting any light to it."

"Just leave everything to me," the R.A.F. man

replied, "and we'll try and get a bit of Anglo-Australian co-operation between the senior and junior services!"

Syme slept well in the mild temperature of a May night.

Next day everything went very much to plan. The weather was rather oppressive, but despite this the manual labour was completed during the forenoon, and the stage was set for the onslaught. "I think I'll wait till midnight before I start," Syme told the S.C. over lunch. "It's best to let the night set in. No point in rushing it about 2100 or 2200. This is the plan I propose. As the mine's mighty close to your huts, I'm afraid I'll have to ask you to provide some alternative accommodation for the men to-night—either all night or for an hour or so. In case of accidents, you know. I'm not an expert yet at this sort of game."

"Yes," came the reply, "we can't risk anything, although it's pretty cold-blooded for me to be looking at it like this. I'll clear all the personnel out for as long as it takes. They'll just have to crowd into that small hut at the other end of the field. Won't hurt them for a couple of hours. I'm sure no one's going to grumble when they realize that you'll be in a far less comfortable position! If we get any complaints we can always hustle them along to change places with you!"

Both of them laughed.

"It shouldn't take too long," Syme said optimistically. "Meanwhile I think, as we are so conveniently situated, it would be a good idea if you could rig up a telephone, and I'll keep in touch with you. Just a routine precaution. Things should go all right, but the Huns are altering their ideas so much just now that it's all we can do to keep up with them."

"I'll arrange it. Don't worry about a thing. Why not try and get a rest? I'll meet you outside here at 2345."

It was ten to twelve—and pitch-black. The night seemed stiflingly close. The wires of the barrage balloons faded into the sky, giving no hint of what floated on their ends. Nothing moved. Seventy degrees Fahrenheit as Syme's watch moved on to midnight.

"Damned hot to-night," he said to the S.C. "I'd better take my watch off. Will you keep it for me?"

"Here's your field-phone. Just walk out with it, and the wire will unwind. I'll be at the other end all the time, if you want anything. Best of luck, old boy."

"Thanks."

Syme strolled over to the mine, leaving a trail of wire behind him. He adjusted the phone and called up the S.C.

"We're all with you in spirit," the S.C. reassured him. Syme thanked him once again. However sincere their wishes, he was on his own now. It was 0004. He sweated gently.

"I'm taking the nuts off now. One . . . two . . . fourteen . . . twenty-two . . ." The minutes passed, punctuated only by the bald statement of the number of nuts unscrewed. Was the night getting hotter? Or was it just himself? Syme wondered.

"Last nut now. I'll get down to that blasted cell in a moment, and you can all go back to bed by about one o'clock."

Far off he heard a faint rumble.

"Sounds as if there's another raid somewhere."

"Long way off," soothed the S.C. "Don't worry about it."

"Nuts all off," reported Syme. "Won't be long now. D'you reckon that's a bomb or ack-ack? Seems to be getting a bit nearer. Still, we've got our own worries to-night. On with the motley, and off with the dome."

Syme eased the large manganese-steel dome away from the mine. In the wan light he could hardly see the far side of the dome. He felt round its rim with his fingers, and pressed it off slowly, taking care not to shake the shell more than he could help. In a second or two he found himself standing upright with the dome in his hands. He laid it down on the grass. He still felt hot.

"Dome removed," he breathed over the phone. "I'm just going to wipe my hands; seem to be sweating. Then I'll get at the switch-gear. I shan't be a second. Don't want to leave it too long. These blessed photo-electric cells are wide open to the night now. Damn dark it's come over. Look at that cloud," he added, as he dried his hands on a cloth, so that the tools would not slip.

The S.C.'s voice came back again: "You're safe on a night like this, anyway, Syme, old boy."

"Something in what you say, I suppose. I'm going to unscrew the switch-gear now. Got to break both circuits of the thing before the cells are safe. Don't want 'em to go off at sunrise!"

Suddenly, as he spoke, from out of nowhere an almighty flash filled the skies. Another. And another. Black clouds above spat lightning into the night. Half-seconds of hell.

Syme stood still as death. Silhouetted beneath a blaze of light. A rugged frame rooted to the spot. This is it. No use running. Can't get away. Wait for it. Twist— or bust. No choice. Every flash a blow below the belt. He reeled, waiting for the knock-out.

Thunder rolled round the field. The grass quivered under his feet.

"My God, it'll go up!" shouted the S.C. "Run, man, quick!" Syme stood his ground.

Another fierce fork slashed the skies. It was light as day for a moment. The mine sat still. A barrage balloon burned at the other end of the town. A final fling of lightning. He was alive.

The storm died as soon as it had come.

Dark again. Syme breathed again. Sixty seconds it had lasted. He did not remember breathing once in that time.

"No wonder I'm sweating," he called over the phone. "That must have been brewing for quite a while."

But the S.C. had not heard. He was running as hard as he could out to see Syme. "Thought you'd gone that time, old boy," he gasped, gripping his hand.

"Frankly speaking, so did I," admitted the abashed Lieutenant.

Back at *Vernon* the scientists pronounced their verdict on the adventure. "From what I hear over at West Leigh House," Ouvry told Syme, "you're lucky to be with us. The lightning just didn't last long enough at a stretch to operate the cells, otherwise——"\ He left the sentence unfinished. "But I'm more glad than I can say that you got away with it."

Syme and Mould both won the George Cross—for this and other work.

I

9

Anglo-American

By June 1942 Britain was really on the offensive in the mine war. And Roy Edwards, meanwhile, had become a bit of a legend, dealing defensively with the enemy's concoctions. For two and a half years since his initial exploit on the East Coast late in 1939 he had roamed the beaches to order after German buoyant mines, either broken free from their moorings and washed across the North Sea or laid offensively off our shores by E-boats and others. He had been specially trained to tackle these standard buoyant contacts, and acted as instructor in the art to all and sundry drafted to Nore Command for brief periods to be taught the techniques. Edwards made his headquarters at Yarmouth, where he had set up a little museum of trophies, which he liked to show to visitors with the justifiable pride of the big-game hunter who had ventured into realms beyond normal experience. As he stood in this room overlooking the East Coast and surveyed the scene all the individual incidents seemed to merge into one endless stream—of waves breaking over beaches and mines lying in every conceivable position. Mines, mines, still more mines. This was the life, he thought on June the 10th, as he chalked up his recent register of successes.

A knock came at the door. He turned, sharply. He was nervy, although he was not aware of it.

"Lieutenant-Commander Edwards, sir?" He heard the soft, slurry, yet attractive tones of a young American.

"My name's Howard, sir. Ensign Howard."

"Why, of course. I've been expecting you. Admiralty told me you were coming up for a spell. Nice to see you, and glad to know you. And glad you Yanks are well and truly in it now."

"No more than we are, sir."

"You've come at a most propitious moment actually," Edwards went on. "I've had a report in only an hour or so ago that there's a Jerry mine ashore at Garton, near Lowestoft. And from the description it's almost bound to be a magnetic. I've been waiting a long time for this chance. Those blessed contact chaps have been boring me stiff lately. Must have been more than a hundred of them by now. But I've never managed to get a crack at a magnetic till now. You're here to learn the tricks of the trade, I take it, so I suggest there could be no better initiation for you than this."

"Sure thing, sir," the American said eagerly.

First thing the following morning Edwards picked up Howard in a lavish limousine which a well-wisher had put at his disposal for the previous year or two. They drove down to Garton. The mine was a buoyant, like so many others he had handled. But it was also magnetic, and needed special attention. Edwards started to show the Ensign the successive steps to be taken to ensure its safety.

The coastguard on the cliffs saw, and heard, the blinding burst on the beach. He raced to the spot, stood heaving brain blurred with the strain of the run. Nothing could be done. Both of them lay dead. On the very beach on which Edwards had handled his first mine.

"Poor old Edwards," said Anderson, at West Leigh.

"Yes, poor old Roy," agreed Ouvry softly. "I was turning the pages of the 'fireworks' book this morning and came across something that gave me quite a jolt." Ouvry pushed a piece of paper across the desk to Anderson. "I was going to try and keep a record of signatures—in case of accidents."

Anderson glanced down at the slip Ouvry had offered him, and swallowed involuntarily as he saw the names. "I remember this, John. Must be a couple of years ago now since these were scratched down." He looked again. The square, direct hand of G. A. Hodges; then the middle one of the three, Roy Edwards, with the initial R and E following a similar pattern. And then a minute detail that brought the whole tragedy flooding back to him with the full force of reality suddenly realized. Under the name, Edwards had traced an underline back left from his final 's,' and then retraced another stroke to the right lower still—but the pen had scratched at this last line, and all that remained as record were four dots in a neat little row.

Four dots. Oh, God—what was the point of it all? How much did a man have to endure? Edwards had done his share, and more. Far, far more. And now four dots on a sheet of crested notepaper seven and three-eighths of an inch deep and four and five-eighths wide. The last stroke. Edwards' epitaph.

Anderson read below the dots. There, characteristically last, was the strong, distinguished style of his boss

—John G. D. Ouvry. Style, with reserve, without flamboyance.

He nodded, thanked Ouvry, and handed the names back to him for safekeeping. It was a hot summer day

in mid-June. But the War was not yet won. Death still amid life. And life amid death went on for Mrs Edwards and the children.

Midsummer, almost all summer, indeed, had passed. Lorna stooped down in front of the door-mat, twisting her head round to see the envelope lying there. It stood apart from the other two rather uninteresting-looking buff bills. She was sure they were bills. She had come to recognize them only too well. They seemed to come at an ever-increasing tempo as the end of a quarter approached, arrived, and passed, finally reaching a crescendo about the first week of October, January, April, and July.

But the letter on its own was different. She picked it up first, tucking the others underneath, ostrichlike, and bore all three into the dining-room, where Ouvry was already attacking a reconstituted egg.

"American postmark on one of them, John," she murmured in her beguilingly absent-minded voice that was entirely unaffected.

"I wonder who—— The writing's not familiar."

He slit the thin blue envelope with his bread-knife. The red, white, and blue edging frayed into a crazy braid. The envelope lay discarded on his side-plate, its duty done—like Edwards'. And Howard's.

"It's from the American boy's mother," Ouvry said suddenly as he scanned the contents.

"How terrible that must have been for her!" Lorna sympathized. "So far away, so remote. Just a letter."

Ouvry had written her a personal condolence as soon as he had heard of the affair.

"What does she say, John?"

"Not a lot, really. She thanks us for writing. Seems to have appreciated it. I felt so helpless, though. What could I say?"

"It wasn't your fault, John."

"No."

"Anything more?"

"Yes," he said slowly. "Yes, there is. What a wonderful thing for her! She says that Knox, he's the Secretary for the Navy over there, Knox has just notified them he is naming a small warship after the boy. She says she is honoured, and it's made them both feel better —her and his father. The U.S.S. *Howard*. That's to be the name of the ship."

Ensign Howard and Roy Edwards live on aboard the ship. An Anglo-American alliance beyond the bounds of space and time.

10

Dive Deep

FROM the first it was clear to Ouvry that Enemy Mining Section could not always expect to find their specimens washed up conveniently high and dry, waiting for inspection like a guard of honour. So the order of the day was: "Go out and get 'em—wherever they are." And the area in which it was most likely to find them, when not on the beaches, was the water. So into the water E.M.S. went. In all sorts of surroundings, and in depths from one fathom upward—or downward! To tackle a mine under water the special fitting had been developed in 1940 for making it safer to handle by the diver doing the job—the thing that Tawn had successfully used in Poole Harbour. But many other hazards remained, not least the inevitable inconvenience of working in the dark, as it were, with the living water all around, constantly stirring the sea-bed—even if only a fraction.

At this stage, too, in the spring of 1941, the *Vernon* divers still relied on their breathing-supply from up above in the ship, by an air-line. It was not until later that an air-supply became self-contained in the diving-suit. Now the diver still had to trail his pipe around with him, an additional handicap in the already-more-than-hard-enough fight.

As soon as the first report came through that a parachute mine had been dropped in the inner harbour at Falmouth it became clear that once the mine had been found the recovery and rendering safe would have to be by divers. A Dornier aircraft flew in over Falmouth one Saturday afternoon, released five bombs on the fishing town, and laid its mine on the return run.

Back at *Vernon*, Commander M sent for Lieutenant J. F. Nicholson, R.N.V.R. "This looks like a case for the divers, Nicholson," he pronounced, "but before we get them on the job you'd better go straight down to Cornwall in advance and try and locate the thing with that echo-sounding gear of yours."

Nicholson had introduced his apparatus into the Navy at the beginning of the War for locating objects on the sea-bed. It was large-scale gear capable of reading depths to as close as three inches. Since this method of location had been brought into service at the end of 1940 a great deal of research and development had been carried out by Commander D. H. Macmillan, R.N.R., in conjunction with scientists in *Vernon*, to increase the range of search, and also to discriminate between metallic and non-metallic objects of similar size located on the sea-bed. This process saved much time and energy previously expended in sending down divers to examine useless objects. Research was further extended to developing a craft fitted with a type of silent propulsion which would be immune from any known sound frequency that was likely to be used in an enemy acoustic mine.

The result of this latter research was a small motor-launch aptly named *The Mouse*, fitted with Hotchkiss propulsion and without a propeller. The launch was given extensive tests over acoustic sea-ranges at all possible speeds and depths, and proved to be a hundred per cent. efficient.

This was the launch that Nicholson accordingly arranged to have transported by road to Falmouth, complete with the detection gear. For the first job was to find the mine, then try to make it harmless.

He and his coxswain, Petty Officer Benham, arrived at Falmouth on the Monday morning, and after consultations with officers of the Naval Base as to the approximate position at which the mine was observed to have dropped, they went into action aboard *The Mouse* at once.

After only half an hour's search several very clear echo-sounding signals of the mine were recorded. These showed it to be in fifteen feet at low water on the bed of a narrow channel of the harbour. As soon as the mine was located a marker-buoy was dropped near it, and moored by a rope attached to a lead sinker. Lead was always used in this kind of operation to offset the danger of exploding a magnetic mine by a metal more responsive. The position was also fixed by sextant angles, in case the marker-buoys were carried away by chance before work could be commenced on the mine by divers.

Nicholson had done his job thoroughly. "You'll want to have our progress report, sir," he said to Commander M over the phone the same afternoon. "We've located and marked the mine, and are now waiting for further orders."

"Capital, Nicholson. You've certainly worked wonders with that gear. I'll get Sutherland, Tawn, and Wharton down there at the first possible moment."

Sub-Lieutenant Sutherland was a diving officer, and

Tawn and Wharton were seamen highly experienced in diving and rendering mines safe under water. The idea was for them to make the mine harmless at Falmouth, and then have it transported back to *Vernon*, where it was wanted to be checked for any new firing circuit.

Silence was golden, was life itself, to anyone attempting to tackle an acoustic weapon, and this could well be one. The three of them knew as much as they headed for Falmouth. In fact, a silence had already fallen on the group for most of the way.

Sutherland had done quite a bit of diving, but he was not so experienced as the two A.B.'s. He was a one-ringer R.N.V.R., a volunteer. He had no close relatives —one reason why he had taken on the job. It was not the sort of thing for a family man.

His mind wandered as the road wound its way south-westward. Where was this thing which lurked for them? Which one of them must encounter and overcome it on the bottom—like some strange sea-serpent that never moved, yet could unleash death in the decimal of a second. Where was it? He remembered the latitude and longitude mentioned on the message received from Cornwall. 5 degrees W. And 50 degrees 10 minutes N. Bang on the longitudinal! He looked at the road map in the untidy little compartment beside the dashboard of the car. 1 degree W., Havant. A quirk of coincidence. 2 degrees W., Poole, where Tawn had handled the first mine under water almost a year before. 3, 4, and 5 degrees. Here they were on the most westerly meridian of England.

They reached Falmouth in the early afternoon of Tuesday. Nicholson met them, and they wasted no time. A diving-boat with a civilian crew was procured, and Sutherland went overboard by the buoyed object to investigate and identify for certain.

A few minutes later he surfaced, confirming to Nicholson, "Yes, it's a mine all right, and the parachute's still attached to it. It's lying in very soft mud, that's the trouble, though. Visibility down there is almost nil: the mud stirs up at the slightest step."

Nothing more could be done that day, but arrangements were made to have an acoustic sweeper fitted with Kango hammers (to explode the mine at a safe distance if it were an acoustic) run near it the next morning. If this did not fire the mine it might be assumed to be magnetic only, and a little easier to tackle than a live acoustic on the sea-bed.

It promised to be a fine day. But a breeze sauntered in from the Atlantic. The hammer sweep was duly carried out at varying distances from the mine, without any effect whatsoever. All the morning the little company were waiting for the possible shattering crack to rend the air of the sleepy harbour. But no.

"As it hasn't responded to acoustic treatment, I feel easier about the job now," Sutherland said to Nicholson over lunch. "I think it's more than likely to be magnetic, so I suggest we go ahead afterwards."

Diving arrangements were laid on for the same afternoon in fairly fine weather.

Nicholson towed the diving-boat into position over the site of the mine with *The Mouse*. The wake of the two little craft rippled away into nothingness. Sutherland donned his diving-suit and tied the tools necessary for tackling the thing around his waist so that he could get at them easily. He descended, leaving Tawn and

Wharton in charge of the telephone and guide-rope on the diving-boat, in company with the minimum crew possible.

Nicholson then took *The Mouse* away with all unnecessary 'hands'—two, in addition to himself—to a safe distance in case of accidents. The Lieutenant eyed the scene anxiously from his vessel. He would rather have been with the divers, but he knew that it was foolhardy for him to invite trouble.

The wind was blowing slightly stronger now, but still the sun warmed the scene. The minutes ticked by. Nicholson rapped the rail of *The Mouse* with his knuckles. He glanced over the two hundred yards or so of water to the Customs House Quay, where a knot of old fisherfolk gossiped the afternoon away. He saw the white clay pipe of one of them bright for a second as the sun dodged between the clouds. They did not know that the diving-boat was aiming at the biggest catch ever seen in Falmouth. Nicholson looked at his watch. Nearly half an hour Sutherland had been below.

Suddenly a small splash sounded near the diving-boat, and Sutherland surfaced. Nicholson took *The Mouse* alongside again to see what there was to report.

"How did it go?" he greeted the Sub.

"Found it again easily enough. And I've had time to get a good look around. It's on the edge of a narrow channel, and still in thick mud. The clock and detonator are on the underside, so I can't work on it as it is lying. I've made a line fast to the parachute-ring, so do you think you can possibly turn the mine over by towing it?"

Nicholson shrugged. "Not too keen on the idea, old

boy. I don't think we'll gain much by it, but I'm willing to give it a try—provided we use a good length of tow-line."

This was managed, together with a more powerful motor-launch, and the strain taken on the tow-rope for about ten minutes. The launch did not appear to have moved ahead any appreciable distance during the tow, and whether the mine moved at all was not known.

After this operation Sutherland said to Nicholson, "I'll have another go now, if you're agreeable." He prepared to make his second dive, Nicholson and *The Mouse* standing by waiting to hear by the telephone that he was safe before taking the little craft off again.

The thin metallic voice came up aloft to the diving-boat: "O.K. I'm on the bottom."

Sutherland stepped carefully. One false move, and . . . but the channel had been swept. That was a comfort. But it should still be live. No reason to know otherwise. The thing had been dropped only three or four days earlier. He was in about three fathoms, but it might just as well have been in three hundred. He was utterly alone. Three times the height of a man from the surface. The sea moved to and fro, barely perceptibly. Merely a heave. His feet stirred the mud into a mist that hung around the mine before settling again. He gripped the cap-fitting in his hand, ready to fit over the fuse. After that all would be easier. But at the moment, assuming that the mine were not magnetic but acoustic, the slightest sound could kill him. He groped forward with the cap, fitted it to the fuse. But as the two touched a slight sound was inevitable. A low-pitched note on the sea-bed. Nothing more. One note at 250 cycles of sound. The microphone in the mine picked it up; a current surged through its circuit; a switch was made; primer and detonator fired. . . .

Sea spurted skyward. A column of water two hundred feet high. An eruptive explosion. A semicircle of spray. Nicholson and his two sailors in *The Mouse* were blown headlong into the water. Seconds later it settled. The mist cleared. All that remained was a mirror-flat circle where the water had convulsed. Nothing of the two boats but a few pieces of stray wood floating free.

Sutherland, Tawn, and Wharton, with the three others in the diving-boat, were all killed. *Vernon* had paid the price.

But the action was not over. The mine fired a furlong from the Customs House Quay, where a motor-launch lay with its motor running. The shock of the explosion threw the coxswain of the launch forward on top of the gear-lever. And by so doing the vessel was set in motion. By an amazing coincidence its bows were headed in the direction of the accident. When the cox managed to pick himself up he realized that the launch was heading straight for the three survivors in the water.

Nicholson and the two others were struggling, and suffering from fractures and shock. Whether they could have held out much longer is hard to say. But by the act of providence of the cox starting the rescue-launch they were all picked up in time. The mine went off at 1740. They were in hospital and their injuries receiving attention by 1800. All in twenty minutes.

It was subsequently ascertained that the Kango hammers in the minesweeper had not been working efficiently. The assumption was clear. The mine was acoustic, not magnetic. Sutherland had had scant chance. Six precious lives were lost, three of them vital men experienced in diving. The mine war was not being won without its losses. *Vernon* was proud of those who perished.

About this time, too, the situation at Suez became critical. The enemy started laying parachute mines in the canal, a vital communicating link, at a number of points along its 105-mile length. All traffic was suspended for dredging and salvage operations to clear a passage through the canal.

Lieutenant-Commander M. W. Griffiths, R.N.V.R., and Petty Officer N. L. Smith were drafted to Suez with instructions to counter the mine menace there. A mine-watching organization was put into working order, in collaboration with the Egyptians, and sweeps were hastened from other areas. Diving-gear and pumps were requisitioned from Alexandria, and suitable boats at Port Said and Suez were brought to bear in systematic searches on the canal bottom by diving-parties trained by Smith. Six or seven mines were located and "countermined" by charges being placed against them which blew them up. Griffiths, meanwhile, was organizing a couple of local Admiralty drifters with reinforced trawls for recovering a mine if the occasion was opportune.

On May 12, 1941, the first signal success was achieved by these trawls. Already two mines had exploded when trawled. On a sweltering day of over 100° F., fanned only by the slightest of desert winds, the steam drifter *Landfall* was trawling over a reported mine near Toussoum, ten miles south of Ismailia, when her trawl picked up a suspiciously heavy weight about the spot given by mine-watching parties. The skipper had the ship's bows

turned in to the west bank of the canal until the fore-
foot grounded on the shore. The trawl, with its weight,
was streamed astern for some eighty fathoms in thirty-
five feet of water. On going aft to lift the net by hand
the crew reported that it had jammed.

Lieutenant Vine, R.N.R., skipper of *Landfall*, volunteered to swim down and examine the situation from
close quarters. A few minutes later he popped up and
announced between breaths, "Looks like a big bomb,
white or pale blue." This was enough. A snatch-block
was rigged on the nearest bollard ashore to lead the
trawl well clear of the drifter's stern. And in case of
detonation while the mine was hauled past the ship the
engine-room hands were cleared, and all hands, in fact,
ordered forward. Hauling commenced.

This was not easy, though, as the net by this time had
jammed once more, over the rudder-head. The whole
ship's company were anxious to see the thing anywhere
else than where it was! Working with a united will, they
managed to haul it to a point about forty yards south of
the vessel. With a final heave it was beached. At that
very second Griffiths arrived in response to a signal from
the ship and hastened to make a sketch of the mine—
"just in case it explodes." Every one was cheered up at
this!

A phone-call to Ismailia R.N. Base brought Lieutenant
G. D. Cook, a Canadian, on the scene with Major
Thompson, of the Royal Engineers. The bomb-fuse was
removed as the sun set over the desert. Griffiths said
suddenly, "Wait a minute, chaps. I've heard from home
that these things may have booby-traps in them, so
we'll have to be blessed careful."

When they had opened it up they found a pair of glass

K

windows inside, which they cleaned and gazed through to see the works inside. "Fascinating," breathed Cook, "but I wonder what these windows are for?"

"Not to worry," Griffiths consoled him. They carried on with the job without further ado.

Jamieson, an R.N.V.R. two-ringer, rushed on to the scene to help with the specialized side of the stripping.

"Hello, Jamieson, old boy!" Griffiths welcomed him. The response he got was hardly expected.

"My God, it's a miracle you three are still in the land of the living! Those windows of yours are photo-electric cells. Once the cover is off, one stab of daylight, and you all ought to be drawing your harps from stores! The signal came in just before I left base this morning. All mining officers are warned that Jerry's dropping these things in Britain—and here, it seems—so that if any mug tries to open them up, zing go the strings of his heart!"

As Dr Atkinson, an Admiralty scientist, told Griffiths rather more prosaically in Alexandria later, "The reason why that mine of yours did not detonate on being dismantled is most obscure, Griffiths, most obscure!"

Thompson, Griffiths, and Cook had a drink back at base in Ismailia to celebrate their escape.

"To the failure of photo-electricity!" toasted Thompson.

"What an amazing contrast!" Griffiths said suddenly. "I've just remembered an anecdote an old friend of mine told me about Suez in the Great War. I never thought I'd be out here—and mucking about with mines, just like he was."

"Tell us all about it," Cook urged.

"Yes, go on," Thompson added. "We've got a whole evening to kill. It can't take that long."

"Well, if you really want to hear about him. But it *is* a pretty lengthy tale. So settle back, and we'll order another bottle of Ismailian beer."

The trio lounged comfortably in the hot dusk of a May evening in 1941. Not half-way through one war, and reminiscing about another—on the self-same spot, practically a quarter of a century earlier.

"Macdonald's the chap's name. Captain Macdonald. He got the D.S.O., same as John Ouvry this time. The contrast I meant just now is this—between the primitive methods of 1915–16 and the Germans' photo-electric cells.

"When Macdonald first came out here, in the early months of the War, the canal was the quintessence of neutrality. ["Good word," interposed Cook.] So much so that a dozen German merchantmen sought sanctuary at Port Said. They were moored together only about fifty yards from Macdonald's ship, the *Minerva*, and their libertymen returning on board used to dwell beneath the bows of the British ship and sing German patriotic songs, until driven off by lumps of coal that our matelots stored on the fo'c'sle."

"What damned cheek!" exploded Thompson.

"Soon after this, though," Griffiths went on, "we proclaimed a protectorate over Egypt, and the canal, of course, lost its neutrality. The German ships had to leave. They didn't seem at all keen on the idea, however, and protested that they were short of stokers. But these were provided, and the ships eventually sailed. This is the first funny part of the story. Outside the three-mile limit the ships were solemnly met by H.M.S.

Warrior and a couple of destroyers, who captured them and escorted them to Alex. If I'd been a German I'd have been furious—but they didn't seem too perturbed.

"A little later the canal and the towns and the French 'gares' were taken over by the Army."

"Good show!" enthused Major Thompson, sipping a lukewarm beer.

"Well, fortunately, both the military and the French officials of the canal company exercised the greatest tact, and there was never the slightest scene, although we entrenched their canal-banks, regulated their shipping, commandeered their tugs and small craft, and threw several pontoon bridges across the canal.

"The canal, then as now, was vital, but experts said that it was impossible for a Turkish army to cross the waterless wastes of the Sinai Desert. Although our Arab agents reported troops assembling at Damascus, we didn't really believe them, never dreaming that they would embark on such a wild idea. We had no planes at all at that time, apparently, so Gurkha look-outs were perched on the signal-posts of the various canal stations, gazing into the desert for an enemy they never expected to see.

"Macdonald used to say that the Egyptian side of the canal was lightly entrenched from Port Said to Suez, while half a dozen posts were established on the Asiatic side, which led Lord Kitchener to ask if they were defending the canal, or it was defending them!

"This is only a bit of background history for you all; filling in the gaps in your neglected education. The upshot of the land war was that our armies eventually advanced across the Sinai Desert to take Jerusalem, and in 1918 to annihilate the Turks in Palestine and Syria.

"Long before all this, though, our enemies and ourselves realized the importance of the canal. And this is where the mine rears its head again. We expected that the enemy would do their utmost to block it by sinking ships. The thought of this didn't disturb the dauntless British, I'm glad to say, as the canal company had guaranteed to dredge a passage round any sunken ship in twenty-four hours. Not bad for those days, eh?

"To frustrate minelaying, however, and prevent Arab spies swimming the canal—not the Channel—we commandeered steam launches and tugs belonging to German and Austrian shipping firms, armed them with three-pounders and machine-guns, and fitted them with steel plates. These craft patrolled the canal by night, searching the banks and intervening waters with lamps borrowed from cars in Cairo. Macdonald commanded this small force, which bore the impressively pretentious nomenclature of Canal Defence Flotilla."

Griffiths paused for breath and beer.

"But soon afterwards, just when he was getting things well organized, the ships were wanted for the Dardanelles, and were replaced by a fleet of American-built launches, fast and efficient.

"Macdonald stationed these in pairs throughout the canal, and kept them for minesweeping. And they picked up every mine that was laid, except one in the Little Bitter Lake that sank a Blue Funnel steamer.

"This is where the story assumes a certain touch of the fantastic. The enemy minelaying was a commendable performance, and the credit for it due to a German spy, whom the British knew as Frank. This man had lived for some twenty years in the Sinai Desert, learning the various Arab dialects, discovering the ancient wells, and seeking the best route for an army to advance—avoiding the age-old track along the northern coast.

"His mining-party consisted of about eighteen Arabs, mounted on swift steeds—camels, of course—who carried a couple of mines in sections, water in goatskins, and kerosene in tins. They used to set out from Damascus, pass through Beersheba, and then strike out straight across the desert. When they were about ten miles from the canal they would halt, put the mines together, fill the now empty kerosene-tins with sand, to be used as sinkers for the mines, and inflate the goatskins to float the mines out while laying. Come to think of it, you couldn't get anything more ingenious than that, could you? Not even these little cells we've been introduced to this week.

"Then, under cover of darkness, silhouetted against the deep desert skyline, they would steal quietly away to the canal banks, select a spot between our posts on the Asiatic side, float out the mines into midstream, slip the sinkers, and the job was done.

"What they didn't know—and luckily never found out —was that at sundown the entire bank on this Asiatic side from Port Said up to Suez was smoothed down by camels, donkeys, or mules dragging a plank behind them! Upon examination, should the bank appear as if it had been trampled on, old Macdonald was notified at once by phone, when the nearest pair of boats would straightway be ordered to sweep the vicinity. So in every case the mines were recovered and destroyed. Except that once where the coast was rocky and the footprints were not seen.

"Once, and once only, moreover, the enemy mining-party were seen returning from their mission, and a patrol of Hyderabad lancers gave chase. But Frank and his Arabs mounted on their camels travelled much too swiftly in the deep sand for the lancers' horses.

"And, of course, Frank escaped—as he always did."

The scene shifts: from one war to another, from Suez back to England.

After the affair at Falmouth, though not as a result of it, the need became apparent for a self-contained diving-suit to undertake recovery operations.

To Anderson and Mould, therefore, fell the duty of developing such a suit. Mould, one of the four Aussies, and a fellow with a big build, in time became the greatest of this diving fraternity. The design of diving-suit developed at Teddington research laboratories incorporated an oxygen-supply carried on the back, independent of air-lines from diving-boats—free of all fetters, in fact, for the operations which wanted all a diver's concentration without worrying about an external air source that also hampered his movements. Mould and Anderson had to be subjected to exhaustive—and often exhausting —trials in the tank before the right mixture of air was finally evolved. And, the most favourable formula having been discovered, trials had to be conducted at different depths, as air and oxygen can create equally different effects at these divergent depths.

To counter any possible powers a diving-suit might have on a magnetic mine, moreover, the design omitted all steel, and used only non-magnetic metal, for such parts as the helmet.

Goldsworthy too, another of the Australians, played a prominent part in these trials, from which was eventually evolved an ideal suit. The design proved itself over and over again in subsequent underwater operations.

Goldsworthy it was who, in April 1944, just a matter of weeks before D-Day, found himself diving after an acoustic specimen in Milford Haven Harbour. Everything was going very much to plan. He pulled on his guide-rope to signify that he wanted to surface. Slowly he was hauled up. A fair swell was running—it was around the time of the spring tides—and the little launch lurched and rolled with the water, tugging fretfully at her anchor. Goldsworthy, rather a small man, but as strong as any in that tough bunch of Aussies, fell foul of the ladder under the boat. He lost his footing, groped for a moment, and hit his helmet against the hull. He hung suspended. A joint came loose. The water poured in. He spluttered. Bubbles from his air-supply shot up to the surface—only a few feet above.

His matelot attendant took one look at the first stream of them, plunged overboard, grabbed him quickly— seconds could cost life—and hauled him clear of the ladder. The rest of the crew got him in. The choking mist cleared. Goldsworthy lay in the bottom of the boat. He opened his eyes. "Thanks, cobber," he flickered. A narrow squeak. All the damage he suffered—a jarred spine.

Mould, meanwhile, had been as busy as ever, one of his now legendary exploits being to tackle successfully *an active acoustic,* when one low-pitched sound would without doubt have killed him.

"Now, are you sure you want to do this one, Goldy?" Ouvry asked Goldsworthy one morning in June. It was a couple of months since the mishap.

"Sure, sir. The spine's O.K., and I want to get cracking again. No good being over here when they're over there."

"Here's the gen, then. But it'll be no picnic, I warn you. You'll sail over in the next available ship to Seine Bay. What we want is another 'oyster'—but we'll be glad of any new specimens you can lay your hands on."

Ouvry was about to elaborate on the 'oyster,' but a rating was clearing his 'in' tray, so he said no more. This was top top secret. The mine must not be mentioned. But they wanted a second specimen badly— and Goldsworthy was going to have a shot at it.

"It's no good my trying to teach you Aussies anything," he went on. "You know it all better than I do now. So good luck and take care. I'd rather see you back here than the mine. We can always try again for that."

So, as the invasion intensified, and after the first German oyster mine had been recovered on land at Luc-sur-Mer, Goldsworthy was sent over to Seine Bay to try to capture under water any new ground mines. Wherever they were, he had to dive for them.

An easy assignment? Hardly anything could have been more harrowing. The beach-heads had been secured, certainly, but shells still dropped in the waters of the bay; mines were being swept and blown up all along the coast; and the allies fired depth-charges regularly to keep the U-boats at bay. Goldsworthy went down amid all these explosions, knowing that if any of them occurred within a mile of him he was liable to feel a fatal effect through the water. He went down. And again. And again. Through the sea throbbed the sounds of war, from far—and near. A mile radius. A sitting target. A stray mine exploded 2000 yards off. It jolted him as he searched at six fathoms. But nothing nearer. Goldy lived. He did not find the oyster—but he lived to dive another day. That was the main thing.

11

Opening an Oyster

FOR the first four years of the War both the Germans and ourselves were developing the top-secret mine of the War—the oyster. Early in 1940 a German Lieutenant-Commander Fett came across an old idea which had been considered in connexion with canal engineering. It was that the change in water-pressure on the sea-bed as a ship moved overhead might be turned to advantage in the form of a device for firing a mine. Fett's suggestion was not well received at first, but later the Germans were persuaded to investigate it. The proposed unit was designed and fitted to a ground mine, therefore, with the intention of its firing as the wave-trough of a ship caused a drop in water-pressure at the bottom. Further experiment, however, revealed that no sweeping anti-dote was possible, and so if such a mine were recovered by the British, copied, and used against the Germans, especially in the Baltic, it could prove a dangerous menace.

The German Air Force and, later, Navy both followed up the idea, and decided that it must be combined with some other firing "trigger." The Luftwaffe produced "acoustic oysters" and the Navy "magnetic oysters." By the end of 1943 both services had workable versions

—but nothing to counteract them. The order, therefore, for assembly of these mines was given, but laying was prohibited, and to be carried out only as a national emergency.

During this time, too, Mine Design Department developed their own oyster along similar lines. The Admiralty, like the German Navy and Air Force, could not find an antidote, but pressed on with perfecting the unit in case it were needed at some stage. Like the enemy's experiments, work proceeded on it under the classification of top secret. The term "pressure unit" was not to be used. The code word was "oyster." M department laid one up at Braystones, a bleak little resort on the exposed Cumberland coast between Barrow-in-Furness and Whitehaven. M's officers ran boats over the unit, which was linked by cable to a little hut ashore containing recording instruments. These tests proved successful, but, apart from the impossibility of sweeping, one further difficulty had to be overcome before the mine could be considered for service. We found, as the Germans were finding at the same time, that swell effect could fire the mine on occasion, so trials were undertaken to record what the sea did on its own to the unit. When this was ascertained the design could be developed further. So the unit was connected to the hut again, and a camera set in motion inside the hut to record the variation in the swell over a period of a week.

Bruce Morton, a young member of the scientific section from West Leigh House, was dispatched up to Braystones, with the straightforward job of changing the roll of film in the camera for another week, and developing the rolls with the records on them.

It was 1943. He caught the 2250 train from Euston. No sleeper eased the journey. The carriage was crowded with Service people. Through the night the train screamed, bound for Barrow in the wan, chill, northern dawn. Morton stepped down to await the little local for Braystones. The express pounded on to Whitehaven, over the same track, but not stopping at Braystones. In came the local for Braystones, a two-coach travesty that throbbed its weird way out of Barrow, and round the great inlet of water to its north. Morton peered out of the compartment. The Cumbrian hills swept down to the rail, to the very edge of this huge backwater. He glanced down the embankment in wonder at billiard-table-smooth bowling-green grass being grown in the water itself. Finer lawn than he had ever seen—deeper, purer. Past Millom and some ominous-looking chemical factories, enclosed and patrolled. Up the Cumberland coastline chugged the nineteenth-century engine, till, exactly opposite the northern tip of the Isle of Man, it panted to a halt at Braystones. Morton shoved the door, and jumped down on to a springy wooden platform. He gathered up his grip as the engine drew breath again. The station clock showed 0904. The stationmaster, also ticket clerk and collector, appeared.

"Mornin', sir."

Morton acknowledged the call, looking slowly round the remarkable setting for this top-secret trial he was absorbed with. "I'd no idea Braystones was bang on the seashore. What a wonderful view!"

"Always been 'ere, sir," replied the railwayman proudly. "And on a clear day you can see full forty

miles straight across to Snaefell, 2000 feet up on the
Isle of Man. It's a sight for your sore southern eyes!
And when you've stepped up the cliffs here you can see
inland to Sea Fell—over 3000 feet that one is."

"It's an amazing place," agreed Morton. "But you
said 'when I've stepped up the cliffs'?"

"Sure, sir. You'll be having your breakfast at the
farm, I hear, like the naval gentlemen who came up last
time."

"That's right. But isn't there a road or something?"

"Landsakes, no, sir! Your only way is up that grassy
cliff there, past the coastguard's, and down the track to
the farm."

Morton thanked him, struggled up the slippery grass
face of the cliff, returned a wave from the coastguard,
and stood atop it in the full force of an early-morning
gale whipped in from the west. The sea and sky seemed
a palette of pastels. The gale blew harder. He put down
his bag a minute, and caught his foot in a grassy rabbit-
hole. He leaned with his full weight into the teeth of the
gale, and it supported him entirely as it flailed up the
cliff-face. Momentarily he hung crazily at 45 degrees to
the vertical, floating in air for all but his feet.

He extricated himself quickly, and followed the cart-
tracks through the field down to the farm.

"Hello, Mr Mor-r-rton," called Mrs Parsons. "We got
your wire, and the parlour's all ready for you. Come in
and get a good meal. You must be famished."

The farm nestled on the side of the hill, facing inland
to the overwhelming grandeur of the Lake District. He
picked a way carefully past the farmyard and into the
parlour.

"Just sit down here, and the girls will bring in your meal."

"It's very kind of you, Mrs Parsons. I hope you haven't gone to a lot of trouble, because I've only got a day up here this time, and there's quite a lot to be done before I get the evening train back."

"Just you relax, Mr Mor-r-rton. You must eat first of all. Nothing comes before that."

Morton sat down expectantly in the neat little front room. The gilt clock shone in the now-and-then sunshine. The pendulum rocked and ticked. Pigs grunted outside the window, and a couple of hens fluttered against the panes.

"Good mornin', Mr Mor-r-rton!"

A sweet, clear young voice heralded a sweeter-still girl smilingly carrying a plate of porridge. "I hope you're hungry. Mummy says you're to eat all this!"

"What's your name?"

"Elizabeth. I'm the youngest. There are two others of us. You'll see them. I'm only fourteen. They're older."

"Thank you, then, Elizabeth. I'll try to manage it all," he said, with one eye on her, one on the pile of porridge. Ten minutes later the door was pushed open by a second tray.

"Good mornin', Mr Mor-r-rton. Did you enjoy your porridge?"

"Good gracious! And what's your name?" asked Morton, more than somewhat surprised to find such beauty and abundance in the wild foothills of Cumberland.

"I'm Rose. And I'm sixteen."

"Thank you very much, Rose. The porridge was delicious."

Rose bore off the plate and replaced it by another filled with several rashers of bacon and two shining orange-and-white eggs.

"Great heavens! I shall go straight off to sleep after all this. We haven't seen such food as this for years!"

Rose bloomed visibly. "I'm glad you like the look of it, Mr Mor-r-rton."

Twenty minutes this time, before a tap on the door announced another entry. Morton was wiping the last of the egg-yolk clean with a fragment of farmhouse bread.

"Good mornin', Mr Mor-r-rton. I'm Fiona."

"Saints preserve us! You're more beautiful than the other two even!"

The girl flushed. She was twenty.

"I've brought your toast and marmalade."

"Thank you, Fiona. You're all being much too considerate."

"Oh—and Mother says you'll want a flask of tea for midday down at the hut. I'll get it for you." And she was gone as quickly as she had come.

Morton bade farewell to them all after breakfast. "I'll be back again in a week or two, I hope." To Mrs Parsons he confided: "If only I hadn't got to go back to-day I'd most likely end up your son-in-law! But don't ask me which one I'd marry: they're all so lovely!"

"They all wanted to give you your meal, so I had to let them each bring in one course to you!"

The four of them waved good-bye as he strode back to the cliff. The wind had dropped a little, and the sky cleared. The Isle of Man rose sheer out of the sea due west—a wondrous sight. The hut was one of a dozen or more used before the War as holiday homes. The cliff sloped down direct on to the railway-line, and the huts stood immediately on the other side, just by the beach. The station awaited the evening train, which would be due at 1810—still seven hours off. Morton clambered down the cliff, hopped over the line, tucked his head between the two wires of the fence, and was on a miniature lawn beside the hut. The paint had peeled off the woodwork of the hut. How odd it all was! he thought. A squat little beach-hut at Braystones, the scene for top-secret trials of the War. Like M's people, they never got near the fighting. It all seemed remote at that instant.

He turned a rusty, unwieldy key in the door. It creaked open. The hut was pitch-dark, so that the camera could record. Its windows were firmly shuttered. He closed the door behind him, blinking at the near-total dark. In a minute or two he saw the thin strip of light which traced the line of the sea's swell on to the paper of the camera. He took the lid off the box-like photographic apparatus; stopped the motor; unwound the rolls of film, one for each day; parcelled them in black paper, and put the package in his pocket.

After an hour or so's adjustments to the gear he groped his way out of the hut and into an even smaller hut next door, where developing materials lay at hand. Crouched double in this four-foot-high hovel, Morton unrolled the first precious roll of film, moved it slowly through the developer, and at long, long last began to see wavy lines appearing. His back ached unbearably. The developing-pan lay on a wooden chair, and his head was bowed over the top of it, touching the back of the chair. He felt sick. The breakfast had been almost too

L

good. The film was not developed yet—not all of it—
nor would be for some time. But he could not leave it
and let in the light. It was all still sopping wet—drip-
ping on to the floor. At last he judged it ready. He
fixed the first roll to a clip on the ceiling, such as it was,
to dry. No good going out of the hut and straightening
up each time he had done one, he decided; better get
them all finished at once. So for hours Morton stayed
cooped up, slowly passing the rolls through the tray of
developer, back and forth, back and forth.

It was mid-afternoon when he finally emerged triumphant with his seven rolls, the earliest ones nearly dry,
the latest still sopping. For several minutes, literally, he
could not stand upright. He hobbled out bent double.
The coastguard lowered his glasses in some surprise.
When Morton did at last force himself up the pain
stabbed through his back. He winced. "Where the
hell can I dry these out?" he asked himself out loud, a
little hysterical after four hours of solitary confinement,
in the dark. He looked at his watch—1610—then
around him to try to find somewhere for the wind to get
at the rolls. The telephone-wires. The very place. The
thin wires would be strong enough to support even wet
paper, weighing a ton, it seemed to him. The twin
strands swooped steeply from the top of the pole on the
railway-line, down to the roof of the hut, where he was
in telephonic touch with the outer world. The wires
went into the hut just by the larger window. Morton
chose a spot above the little lawn to peg his papers out.
He shivered in the breeze which was whistling once
more round the hut. He was glad of his oilskin and sou'-
wester. The rolls should dry easily here. He disappeared

into the hut to reset the camera, fix the fresh rolls of film, and make one or two repairs before quitting. These took more time than he thought. He could hear the wind without. The luminous dial of his watch showed 1715. Under an hour for the train. Nearly through. As he locked the door behind him it was 1722. Three-quarters of an hour. Just nice time to pack everything up and stroll along the single track to the station. He congratulated himself on a good day's work. But he was premature.

He crossed the lawn, and automatically raised his arm to reach the pegged rolls of film from the wires. No sign of them! My God! What the hell! Where? Where? He was alarmed. Suddenly it all assumed the shape of a spy story. He'd lost the top-secret records. How on earth could they have vanished—unless they had been taken? Could an agent have known of the hut at Bray-stones and calmly walked off with them? An awful possibility! Morton scoured the grass verge, and ran along the track, searching the base of the cliff. Nothing. Next he tore up and down the beach scanning the sands for white specks. Again, nothing. He called up to the coastguard, "Did you see any papers blowing about in the wind?"

"Sorry, sir," came back the voice through the self-same wind. "Nothing like that—and I've had my glasses on the beach all the time."

"Thanks, anyway. No strangers about, either, I suppose?"

"Not a soul."

Morton was desperate. The time was 1753, adding to the sense of urgency. Seventeen minutes to train-time. He had to get back south. But he daren't go without

the records. They *would* be top secret, and not just a
routine trial. Sickening. He sat down on the grass,
gazed disconsolately up at the telephone-wires. His
eyes followed the wires, up, up, to the telegraph-
pole.

Something white fluttered right at the top of the
pole. It was a long, narrow strip of paper, flying banner-
like in the breeze. The film! He rushed up the bank,
slipped down again, up a second time, screwed his eyes,
and saw all the other papers rolled tightly round the
pole. The wind must have whisked them up the wires
to the top, where they had got entwined with the main
wires.

He started to climb the metal steps up the pole. But
they did not go far enough. The papers still flew defiantly
out of reach. He jumped down, frantic. 1808. Seven
minutes for the train. He dug his way up the cliff at the
double, up to the coastguard.

"A ladder, you say? Well, I've got an old one behind
here."

Morton was gone, sliding down the cliff again with the
ladder tucked under his arm. He propped it against the
pole, shinned up in giant strides—and grabbed all seven
rolls gratefully. Saved! By the time he had descended
it was 1808. Two minutes to go. The coastguard called
out that he would pick up the ladder. The records were
dry. Bone-dry. Morton rolled them hurriedly into his
bag. He heard a whistle. Beyond the headland—St
Bee's Head, it was—he saw the tell-tale smoke of the
1810 train rising with dignity above the cutting. He
zipped the bag, clambered on to the track. 1809. The
train was dead on time. It was still a half-mile north
of the station. He was 300 yards due south. He ran

along the sleepers, the bag jolting against his side. At 1810, exhausted, he scrambled up one end of the platform as the old train moved majestically into the other. The engine drew alongside him. The driver stared in some incredulity at the figure below him, heading haphazardly for the first compartment. The stationmaster waved twice, once for Morton, once for the all clear. And the Braystones flyer sped southward at a speed gathering to 80 m.p.h.

Such were the trials—and tribulations—of our own mines. We never laid an oyster, but our other circuits were sinking hundreds of enemy ships every year.

Meanwhile the Germans were producing their own oysters, and it was these which were to form the third of the trio of fatal blunders the enemy made during the year of destiny—1944.

Early in the year the Germans were highly conscious of the imminence of an Allied invasion, so as a protective measure a large defensive field of moored mines—blockade of buoyant types—was laid parallel to the coasts of Holland, Belgium, and Northern France. They reckoned for certain that the Allies would invade during the first five months of the year. They could not leave so widespread a minefield indefinitely, as it would interfere vitally with their own vessels plying those seas. Every one of these mines, therefore, was fitted with a sterilizer—or flooder—set for the end of May. The weeks went by, turned into months, and still no invasion came. Then, at various times throughout the day of May 31, each of the thousands of mines in this great field flooded according to schedule, and sank harmlessly, with complete futility, to the bottom. An enormous waste—and a major mistake. Six days later came D-Day. The extent of the error need not be emphasized. Some of them would have been swept, certainly, but the hindrance they would have caused would undoubtedly have resulted in additional casualties.

A bad blunder, yes. But an irrevocable one, no. Added to the second slip, it became serious. As these legions of lost mines sank silently to the sea-beds around the three countries the invasion fleet, an armada of unprecedented magnitude, was assembling at points all along the South Coast of England. Most particularly did it congregate in the Solent, spreading south into St Helen's Roads. For days on end ships were so tightly packed that they could scarcely swing clear of each other with the tide. Here was a chance in a million for the fading fortunes of the Germans. If they had showered only a small number of mines among these vessels alarming results would have been obtained. With so great a concourse at anchor there, the waters could not have been swept, and ships could not safely weigh anchor, or even swing to the tide if mines had been laid.

The Germans did try twice to mine the Solent area a little earlier on—the dates were April 28 and May 15—but the raids produced neither casualty nor inconvenience. On the first occasion white flare markers were dropped in the Needles channel well clear of any anchorage, while a strong tide was running. Minelaying aircraft came over afterwards and dropped their missiles on to the flares, which by then had drifted into shallow water. The result: most of them exploded harmlessly with the lack of depth of water. To make matters still easier, two mines fell on land without exploding at all—at Milford-on-Sea. These gifts were photographed and stripped forthwith by *Vernon*. The mines that did fall in deep water were swept up by acoustic sweepers.

The other minelaying raid was made on the Eastern Solent, but fighters and a smoke-screen completely frustrated the attack, and the only observed mines fell on land. Thus was a golden opportunity lost.

The last of the great blunders of the Germans concerned the oysters themselves—the secret unsweepables which were to be invoked only in emergency. As the spring wore on, and birds nested near Stokes Bay and its amassed armada, the Germans decided that the emergency had come—or soon would come. Two thousand oysters were sent to France, and a further two thousand held in store in Germany and Norway. So great was the secrecy surrounding them that no one—not even senior officers in the Luftwaffe who were to lay them—was instructed in their nature or preparation until April. They were to be laid only on receipt of a personal command from the Fuehrer.

At the beginning of May Goering ordered all oysters to be returned to Germany. This took time, and the operation was not completed until June 4—forty-eight hours only before the invasion. This was a snap decision on Goering's part, influenced partly by German intelligence as to the probable site of the Allied landing. The invasion was expected evidently on the west coast of France opposite the Atlantic. The order was made to prevent the mines stored at Le Mans from being overrun before they could be used. Moreover, oysters were considered of little use in the deep, exposed waters of the Atlantic. The effect of swell would compromise them, and the depth was too great for effectiveness. The decision to return them to Germany was also taken because the rubber bag, part of the unit, had a short life, and was due to be replaced by another made of improved material. So it was that the unsweepable oysters were far away in the Fatherland and unavailable as the assorted landing-craft assaulted the Continent on D-Day—although an order came through from the High Command for their use. The last of Hitler's secret weapons for the sea had misfired. The R.A.F. blasted all communications between Germany and France in early June, so it was nearly a fortnight after D-Day before the oysters could be transported to the Western airfields for aerial laying.

On D plus 14 the first specimen was recovered at Luc-sur-Mer by Sub-Lieutenant Young, flown over from a temporary air-strip to Thorney Island, near Portsmouth, and found to be an acoustic oyster. Immediately counter-measures came into operation. All ships in invasion waters reduced speed. This cut down the casualties.

By the end of July more than two thousand oysters had been laid in Seine Bay, magnetic and acoustic. But they had scant success due to the bad weather producing a swell, which enabled them to be swept by plain acoustic sweepers. The magnetic oysters too were rendered largely ineffective by the combination of slow speed of ships and swell. The Luftwaffe had counted on the period after the invasion being calm weather, with no rough seas. But the pressure, or oyster, side of the firing circuits was actuated by the swell, leaving the minesweepers only the other half to excite, so that the mines might fire safely out of range.

With 1945 the Germans planned a last large-scale attack on British ports, using new oyster mines laid from jet-propelled aircraft, but shortage of planes and fuel ruled out the entire operation. This project was the final desperate throw of a defeated dynasty.

But before this, in the previous autumn, while the Allies still slogged through the Low Countries, John Ouvry was summoned to Belgium to tackle his last batch of mines. . . .

12

Vernon Victory

BRUSSELS was free, but the War was far from won. One evening in mid-September of 1944, a R.A.F. officer caught sight of the bomb-flash on the cuff of a sub-lieutenant of a naval party staying overnight in the Belgian capital. Casually he mentioned to the bomb man that the Air Force had found a lot of unidentified German material at an airfield not far from the city. The Sub followed up this chance intelligence. From their description the weapons sounded as if they might be mines. And Britain still needed to know all she could to ensure keeping the one jump ahead. The winter would soon be setting in. Not many miles away the legend of Arnhem was being written in blood.

What he found near Brussels proved to be a field full of German mines in various stages of readiness or disarray, abandoned before the onsweep of the Allies. He signalled to the Admiralty, who dispatched Ouvry, Lieutenant Broom, R.N.V.R., and Common, a young, tall scientist from Mine Design Department.

On September 24 the trio left Northolt in a Dakota and a full gale. During the two-hour trip across the Channel the transport plane frequently fell through space alarming depths, and interspersed this—for variety—with swaying from side to side. Ouvry's proverbially unsteady stomach he kept under control only by the most rigid discipline he could impose. At 1300 they touched down, not a moment too soon and still bumping, on the rough surface of an impromptu air-strip. The September sky looked leaden, the clouds blown into weird streaks of grey.

The slightly haphazard figure of Common in the Albert Hotel wearing the uniform of a corporal in the Home Guard excited a buzz of Belgian comment and curiosity—the first, and perhaps the last, Home Guard to tread their soil.

Next day they were driven out to Melsbroeck Airfield, where they saw the booty for the first time—rows and rows of mines more or less ready for dropping from aircraft, only there were no aircraft. The Germans had moved out in a hurry.

All three of them had been excited about this trip. They really felt that they were getting the Hun on the run in their own branch of the battle, as, indeed, they were. But it was only when the rows of long cylinders confronted them that the full force of the job sprang to mind. Even then the excitement, élan, and elation outweighed it, but Ouvry did not want any trouble at so late a stage as this.

"Now, look here, chaps; I know you've come over partly for the ride, as I have, too, but it's my responsibility to see that you use the return half of your tickets, so settle down and don't take any risks. This isn't going to be easy by any means. We don't know what state these blessed things are in. One may be live, the next a dud. And don't let's be boobies for any traps that may be going. If we walk carefully and follow the good old manual of instructions we should be all right. The main thing is not to get slack or assume anything's safe till we've proved it."

In the afternoon, having checked the numbers involved and taken a preliminary look around, they tackled the first one or two specimens. They found the latest German circuits all wired up—and unfortunately all wasted, from the enemy's point of view.

Ouvry and Common reckoned to return to England with an advance consignment of material after about three days' intensive work, taking with them any interesting new components or ideas from the mines made safe by that time.

Back at the Albert Hotel, on the night of September 25, Ouvry lay in bed looking up into the still, shrouded room.

The curfew had sounded at 2859. As a liberated city, Brussels was yet young and under military orders. Ouvry did not sleep at once. He thought of the irony of running into anything on the next day, or the next. One never quite knew. And Broom too. He hoped nothing would happen to him. Soon the Wavy Navy chap would be getting demobbed. And Common, what of him, not even in a full Forces' uniform?

Back in 1939 and 1940 he had not stopped to think too much. It was best that way. Then it had all been happening so hurriedly; exciting, in a desperate sort of way. Now their excitement was born through the promise of victory.

It would certainly be the crowning quirk of fate to have dodged everything in the teeth of defeat, and then to buy it within an ace of victory. Then he had not thought. Why? Because there was no choice. Shoeburyness seemed something that had to be done. Now this would probably be the last time he would be called on to touch anything live; and now he had time to think. In a strange, free city. He wanted to live. Who didn't? It would be hard on Lorna if anything cropped up at the eleventh hour. It didn't do to delve too deeply. The course was clear. As it had always been. Two things mattered still. England. The family. Still in that order. It must be the right way round, surely? He asked himself the question, and others, in the black night. Guns groaned a long way off. The dark could play strange tricks.

Next morning he felt fine. Of course it would be all right—and for all of them. They spent a busy forenoon, hampered, however, by the wind and the rain. The words wound round his brain—the wind and the rain, the play at Folkestone before the War by that rep. company, and pretty good too.

Despite the weather, their spirits soared now, bubbling over with confidence. Slowly, surely, one by one, the fangs were drawn. Three, six, twelve. Steady, sustained effort, like a pilot's job on a long-distance bombing raid. No flash in the pan, just hours in the mud with the mines.

Cutlery was short at lunch. "You can have one weapon each, knife or fork, but not both," the Wing Commander told them. Rain leaked in through this most seaworthy—or weatherworthy—of the buildings on the airfield, but they ate with relish. Afterwards the airman led his squadron off to Eindhoven.

The two days following they ploughed on through the mines, making good headway without the rain. And as they worked, at the other end of the field there stood symbolically a Focke-Wulf 189 with its tail at sixty degrees up in the air—crazily crashed nose first into the tarmac. Germany on the downgrade.

Nothing happened to the trio. They survived.

And on the third day they were joined by some Americans, who helped out the operation after Ouvry and Common had left. Broom stayed on to help clear up the rest.

Ouvry and Common were given a Dakota at Brussels Airport for their return trip. The plane was one of the relays being used to convey the wounded from Arnhem, via Brussels, back to Britain.

"I say, we can't take one of these," Ouvry protested to the Station Commander.

"Now, there's no need to feel guilty about bagging one," came the reply. "We've got twice the number we need, and you've got to get back, so just jump in and go right ahead."

So Ouvry, D.S.O., and Common, corporal, Home Guard, came home with the injured of Arnhem—and a mistaken sense of guilt.

Events in Europe came quickly to a climax. For *Vernon* it was a case of clearing the sea-lanes. Over in Veere, on North Walcheren, a special operational diving team under Lieutenant Gray, R.N.V.R., arrived to neutralize a bargeload of mines in the channel. The barge had been sunk by a British plane, and to Gray and his men was entrusted the job of rendering safe all its ninety-nine mines.

Blundell, the Mining Commander, and Ouvry arranged to visit them while making a trip to the *Vernon* mining centre at Ostend. The date fixed for the start of the journey was Monday, May 7, 1945, by a complete coincidence. From the Shetlands down to Suez men and women were beginning to gather ready for the great moment. And on this very Monday morning Ouvry, who had played so priceless a part in making possible the wonderful week that was to follow, Ouvry stood a silent figure in the spring sunshine on Charing Cross Station.

"A great day, John," Blundell called out to him at 0900. "We've waited years for it. Now it's here. So sit back and enjoy it. If anyone deserves it you do."

The two officers faced each other in the compartment. Ouvry lit his pipe and looked out over Hungerford Bridge as the nine-fifteen to Dover drew quietly out. Hungerford, where in 1940 the mine had been fused to the rail. What was the chap's name who did that one? Slipped my mind for a moment. Mustn't let that sort of thing happen. Got a good memory usually. So much to remember, so many men. Gidden, that was it.

Some he would not see again. Ouvry could not crystallize just how he felt. Relief, yes. An overwhelming sense of peace such as he had not known for sixty-eight months.

"The main thing I'm thankful for at this very minute," he told Blundell, "is that sunshine up there. I'm a bad small-ship sailor, as I've been forced to admit on more than one occasion. The prospect of a four-hour Channel crossing in an M.T.B. isn't my idea of an impending end to hostilities!"

The five proud sections of Waterloo Bridge spanned the river with the consummate artistry of creative architecture. An achievement indeed! This was a moment of achievement; of fulfilment. St Paul's stood serene, stone-grey touched with white sun. The old and the new. The metallic rattle and rumble of Hungerford ceased. They were headed south-east.

Blundell flicked absent-mindedly through *The Times*. Ouvry's gaze soared far out over the countryside. Kent came into focus. The front-line country. No more bombs, or V1's, or V2's. Copses were carpeted with the bluebells of May. The tall green banks rose from the railway as the train sped through deep country cuttings. Campions and bluebells blended now into eye-searing splashes of pink-white-and-blue. So to Dover. A poor, proud town, with the castle still standing. A flag fluttered. The train slowed, stopped.

"Good morning, sirs!" A gay little Wren stood beside her equally gay Hillman Minx, waiting to whisk them on board the boat.

"A couple of Minxes," Blundell observed, "but both in the nicest possible way."

"Welcome, you two. You've got the choice of my cabin or the bridge, whichever you like," the Captain called cordially.

"Thanks. We'll settle for the bridge on a day like this," Blundell accepted. "It'll be a change crossing the Channel without expecting the worst all the time."

Magnetic minesweepers passed close by them as they stuck religiously to the swept channel. As these M.M.S.'s drew abeam the M.T.B. Ouvry said, "Hope they don't send one off now. That would be just too much. To fiddle about with the wretched things for five years and more—and then get blown up by our own sweep!" But the water was unruffled, with peace in the air.

1600. Nearly four hours from Dover. "Just look

over there to starboard "—Blundell pointed—"nothing but wrecks. Good job the Captain's keeping his own course."

"He was telling me a ship was mined here only the other day," Ouvry said.

They were outside Ostend now. At 1630, the exact time anticipated by the skipper, the M.T.B. tied up. And at 1635 Blundell and Ouvry stepped on to Belgian soil.

"Hello, there!" Ruttle, an Australian two-ringer, was there to greet them with a jeep. "Am I glad to see you two! Come on, we're going to the Naval Club for tea first of all, then on to the N.O.I.C. After that you can call in at your hotel."

His senior officers had no time to argue. This was to be the pattern of the next two days. Momentous, historic, world-shattering days. Europe was erupting. All the signs they could see about them. At dinner they heard the news of VE Day.

"You can expect excitement from now on," Ruttle told them. "These people have been repressed too long. They'll go mad to-morrow."

Ostend was *en fête*.

"We've certainly picked the wrong day for work, old man," Blundell said to Ouvry, "but don't let's worry. Just let it happen."

Back in the hotel the spirit of victory surged to and fro through the foyer, infecting every single soul in its wake. Soldiers and A.T.S. sang and drank. The *Vernon* pair were quickly absorbed by a collection of cheerful R.N.V.R.'s, who were sinking neither mines nor ships, but whisky galore. And so to bed.

.   .

M

No one else was astir at 0800 next morning when Blundell met Ouvry in the large restaurant of the hotel for a breakfast of fried plaice. Before it was gone they heard the now familiar call from Ruttle.

"The peep of the jeep!" rhymed Ouvry, recovered already from the rather heavy session overnight.

They drove along the much fortified coast, through Blankenberghe, Zeebrugge, Knocke—shades of other days, other wars. Seaside bungalows still bore the mark "Minen," but, this apart, little signs of damage could they see on the Belgian side of the border. Over in Holland ruin was rife. Such shops as were standing seemed to be quite devoid of stock.

It started to rain. The ardour of victory became temporarily dampened. At Breskens they boarded a motor fishing vessel for Flushing. Half-way across the channel suddenly the sky cleared. The water was calm. It seemed hard to realize that just beneath the surface, immediately to port and starboard of the little ship, mines still lurked. VE Day it might be—but they would take time to clear.

As they stepped ashore on Walcheren the sun streamed down on a lone figure hurrying forward to meet them.

"Greetings! Greetings! John Ouvry, my friend! This is a day to remember the rest of our lives." And the Dutch Lieutenant-Commander Mahieu was with them. The sun glinted and glistened in his eyes for a second.

"Hello, Mahieu!" Ouvry called to him. "We always said we'd meet you in Flushing when it was free. How wonderful to be here at the very moment of victory!"

Mahieu led them excitedly through the town—poor and battered, but gay with bunting. Hundreds of women and children disported in orange ribbons which moved mellowly in the May breeze. Smiles, shouts, sobs, cries, sunshine—the élan of Europe.

The four of them—Mahieu, Blundell, Ouvry, and Ruttle—wended a way through to the N.O.I.C.'s office, where they were presented to another Dutch naval officer. "Gentlemen," this newcomer to the group announced with some sense of occasion, "here I have a bottle of Booth's gin for an event which you will witness in a moment. The gin will give you—how do you say it?—some Dutch courage!"

The party grew. They were joined by a colonel of the Royal Engineers. A way was made for them all from the office, out into the town, past the high-flying Dutch men, women, and bairns, to a clearing in front of the famous Flushing landmark—the statue of Admiral de Ruyter. Here they were introduced to the Burgomaster, a fine old white-haired gentleman.

"He has endured five years in a Nazi prison," Mahieu whispered to Ouvry. "It's amazing he is alive, don't you think?"

Ouvry nodded with some solemnity.

A fanfare of trumpets. The Burgomaster clambered on to a large stone block, stood very erect, and with a poignant dignity made a splendid speech in perfect English. He presented a special ensign to the Colonel, representing the British Armed Forces of Liberation. The Colonel stammered a few halting words of thanks. The band struck up the two national anthems. Every one cheered and laughed, bubbling over on this day of days.

"Now you must come with us to my little apartment," insisted Mahieu, and he led Blundell, Ouvry, and

Ruttle along to a snug room in one of the upper storeys of an official building near by.

Ouvry looked round the room quickly. It was meagrely furnished. So much poverty. So much destruction. So much to be done.

"Here on the table, my friends, you will see a tray with a bottle of Lucas Bols Dutch gin. I have kept it all the War for this moment. Will you do me the honour of drinking it with me? It is the anniversary of our wedding-day as well, so, you see, I have everything to drink for—and live for—this day."

The three British officers drank to Mahieu and his wife and their children.

"Thank you, gentlemen. Now you must let *me* have a toast. No excuses, now. I shall insist. John, I wish to remember Mrs Ouvry and your two charming boys, Robin and Philip. They helped me to have hope when I saw them all over in England. I don't know just what it was, or why. Perhaps seeing you as a family. The strength behind it. The reason why we were all struggling. Whatever it was, I always felt better after my visit to your home. A little less alone."

"I know what you mean," Ouvry said. "But look, chaps, I'm about to be a proud papa for a third time! I had to leave Lorna at a bad moment, but any day now we hope to have either a third boy on our hands or a dainty little girl."

"Which do you want, John?" asked Blundell.

"Lorna wants a girl for a change, but I must say I shall be grateful for any small mercy, male or female!"

"Well, this calls for one last toast!" Mahieu was on his feet, seizing the opportunity. "And now we'll go on by car to Veere, yes?"

A group of little girls held up brilliant ribbons for them as they crossed the road. Mahieu grabbed them gleefully, impetuously, and pinned them on to his colleagues' uniforms. There they stayed, as a silent token till the British men left Dutch territory later that evening.

The road ran along beside the canal, and via Middleburgh, the capital of Walcheren. On either side fields and villages lay flooded. A sad sight in a day of gay-and-grey touches.

It was Mahieu's job, incidentally, to clear the German mines and obstructions from the approaches to the four great gaps in the protective dykes—gaps blasted by the R.A.F. to inundate German fortifications. Once done, bargeloads of rubble would be shipped to close the gaps, and when the blocks had been properly reinforced the task of pumping out the flood-water would begin. A long job, but the Dutch were used to such labours.

The car swung into Veere, a sweet little seaside resort, and a haunt of artists before the War. "Painters used to come here a lot in peace-time, I hear," Ouvry said; then added, "But, of course, this *is* peace-time. I'd forgotten for a minute. Peace-time. What a wonderful word!"

They met Gray, who shepherded them quickly into a fine old Dutch building, a species of inn, where a local family were looking after other officers and men with great care. "We've got to hurry," explained Gray, "or we'll miss Churchill." They reached the inn just as the Prime Minister started to speak. A motionless group, Dutch and British, heard the victorious voice on a radio that had been secreted throughout the occupation. At last the utter reality reached them: it was Victory in Europe.

Gray took them out to the bargeload of mines. It was partly uncovered. The deadly cargo lay under-water. They sailed round for a while, and then glimpsed the view of Veere from the water—an idyllic, sleepy skyline, with the inevitable windmill in the foreground to give it atmosphere and perspective.

"No wonder they come to paint the place!" said Blundell in awe. "I think these men of yours are putting one across you, John. They're here for a damned good holiday!"

"Jolly good luck to them, I say," Ouvry retorted with a broad, beaming grin. "The War's over, true, but there'll be a lot of awkward jobs like this to be done for quite a while yet. So if the surroundings help to com-pensate for them, what could be fairer?"

Blundell chuckled. "You don't have to defend the boys to me, John. I know what a rough time they've had—and you as well, for that matter."

Back at the inn, they partook of tea in the main parlour, polishing off some local recipe for lard buns. "Better than the wardroom," said Ouvry decidedly. "And the Naafi ought to take a few tips from these folk!" They bade farewell to their hosts, and made the return journey to Flushing by car, considerably more comfort-able than the jeep on the cobbly, shell-pitted roads of the mainland.

Back at Flushing, Mahieu was waiting for them. "I'm afraid your M.F.V. booked for Breskens has failed, so I've managed to get an M.L. instead." They looked across to the spacious launch, and hustled down into her. But some one must have passed the word around that a free trip over the water was in the wind, for a whole host of local boys and girls—mostly Scouts and Guides

—appeared out of nowhere, screaming with delight. They tumbled down on top of the officers and begged to be allowed to stay for the run. As soon as the M.L. was under way mouth-organs were whipped out magically, as wondrously as the children themselves had come, and the entire episode took on a dreamlike quality. But the music sounded real enough, and soon a party was in progress. To the gentle rocking of the boat and the throb of her engines *It's a Long Way to Tipperary* wafted on to the evening air. The kids gabbled away excitedly in Dutch between the tunes, and Blundell and Ouvry joined in all the choruses with zest. A day indeed! Ouvry's thoughts sped over to another waterway, threaded their way up Portsmouth Harbour to Fareham Creek. How was Lorna? When would the baby be born?

The reliable Ruttle met them on schedule at Breskens, waving from his jeep parked on the quayside—almost in the water. So on to Ostend, through towns *en route* packed with processions and gaiety galore.

"We're in for a rowdy evening by the look of things," Ouvry observed.

"Well, it's only once in a lifetime a war ends—or we hope so," said Blundell. "And even if the Japs are still going strong the worst's over."

The trio reached the hotel at 2015. The dining-room was crowded. The table they had booked was taken long before. Soon they were seated, though, and swung into the spirit of an infectious, inspiriting throng. The noise was deafening. The larger tables started their own favourite songs and tried to drown all rivals. Sweating Dutchmen leapt on to their chairs to conduct their own special songs and collect recruits for their choirs. A ruddy little man did a "William Tell" act. He perched a glass of equally ruddy wine on his head, swayed round deliriously with arms outstretched. Bread-rolls flowed in his direction. One scored a hit—not on the glass, but in his face. Still the wine stayed aloft, with a charmed life. More hoots and shouts. Somehow he clutched at it again before the precious pearls spilt.

Between courses crocodiles of brilliantly, ebulliently bawling Belgians wound their way through the tables. As each cork flew from the champagne the 'pops' produced cheers.

When the trio finally finished their meal Blundell said, "How about a quick dash along to the club, chaps?" So saying, they sped down the street and into the crowded naval club. A two-ringer bore down on them with a rolling gait, got not from the sea, but from the celebrations. "Admiralty orders," he explained ecstatically. "Splice the main brace."

It was 2300. They ran into officers from the base ship —the steam yacht *Sylvano*—who persuaded them to go out into the harbour to their berth to see the zero-hour zenith to the VE delirium.

0001 on the 9th. Peace. Every ship in the harbour switched on a bevy of brilliantly coloured lights—the rainbow after the storm. Rockets shot high into the night air, cascaded sparklingly, spectacularly.

The spirit of man stood free.

Whistles, hooters, sirens—anything that made a noise —whooped jubilantly with one accord. And the steam sirens of the *Sylvano* screamed loudest of them all. Ouvry raced on to the bridge, took over the siren lanyards, and with one in each hand morsed "VE" to the world at large. One world again—almost. Men united.

Men at peace. Some one else was sounding "VE" on the ship's bell.

A final drink—and a toast to the future. "May complete peace come soon," voiced Blundell, "and last for ever!"

He and Ouvry reached their rooms back at the hotel around 0300. By 0315 they were asleep. At 0330 an Army captain strode into each room in turn, insisting that he had booked one of them. After that all really was peace.

Breakfast of fried plaice caught off Ostend was followed by a drive down to the harbour to call on the Commander Minesweeping, Belgium. A morning of business, then Ruttle jeeped them off to Brussels.

Bruges. Ghent. Both were undamaged. Everywhere *en fête.* Thousands and thousands of people they passed, clad in colourful clothes; forming processions, waving flags, singing songs. On to Brussels. The entire population was out of doors. Every one wanted a lift. Ruttle stopped to ask the way. At once two gracious girls begged to come for a ride—wherever they were going. But the jeep was crammed with gear already, and they had work to do. After some difficulty and delay they found the office of the Flag Officer, Belgium. The first person they saw was the assistant secretary to Rear-Admiral Hutton, a supply lieutenant.

"Good news for you, sir," the Lieutenant (S) said eagerly to Ouvry. "I've got a personal message for you which has just come through. A son arrived for you yesterday; mother and child are doing well; *Vernon* (M) send their good wishes and congratulations."

Ouvry was overwhelmed. What a wonderful peace

offering! David, a son of peace. And on VE Day itself. How amazing, astonishing, astounding! Lorna and life were both good.

Ruttle had to leave them, as he was due to make an early start for Dunkirk the following morning to inspect some German explosive motor-boats, now surrendered.

After farewells to him, with thanks for his efficient driving duties, Blundell and Ouvry trekked off to the Rendezvous Club, a magnificent house originally owned by the ex-millionaire Baron Löwenstein, who committed suicide by jumping out of a plane. The place was being run temporarily by the Canadians for British officers, and all the trappings were original. The staff too consisted of the old retainers, who took great pride in showing visitors around their domicile.

"Now I insist on two more toasts," Blundell said authoritatively. "We must drink to David's arrival—and the health of Lorna."

The old grey-haired head-waiter crawled up to the table.

"Bonsoir, messieurs. And what have I the honour of getting for you?" he asked them in that quaintly charming combination of languages that sounds so natural on the Continent.

"We'd like you to recommend the best wine in the cellar, if you'll be so kind," Blundell responded.

"Without the shadow of a doubt, monsieur, it is the Haut-Barsac." The waiter was pointing to a white wine half-way down the list. "By comparison," he continued, with due dramatic pause, "champagne is fifth-rate."

"Haut-Barsac has it, then," said Blundell enthusiastically.

The two men drank the toast. Ouvry wished Lorna had been there at that moment.

After the meal they wandered round the rooms, up broad flights of stairs with the walls hung with Gobelin tapestries and priceless paintings. In a charmingly secluded little vestibule they paused to round the day off with an exquisite liqueur. "Rather amusing," Ouvry observed, as he sipped and savoured the last of his liqueur, "they all look as if they want to have a real binge down there, but I do believe the place is exercising a restraining influence on them."

Certainly the Army officers, with a few A.T.S. and nurses, behaved with dignity, not to say distinction, under the splendid, overawing rooms of the club.

Blundell and Ouvry sauntered sleepily through their midst, down the road, dazzling with victory illuminations.

Thursday, May 10, was Ascension Day, so the shops were closed for a third time in succession. Undaunted, however, Ouvry found a little lace store tucked away off the main street, rang the bell, waited for a reply, opened the door, and walked in. He was greeted by a benign Belgian in pince-nez, who said he would be glad to serve him. Ouvry handled several delightfully delicate pieces before deciding on his purchases, which included a perfect Brussels rose-point lace handkerchief, with a subject the image of an English wild rose.

Together the two officers wandered on through the city. They looked in at the Cathedral, where a Roman Catholic service was in full swing. And at 1500 a car called to take them to the airport, where they were hustled into a Dakota. "To England, home, and beauty! You're a lucky fellow, John."

Ninety minutes later they touched down at Croydon. "Anything to declare?" came the familiar question.

"Only a couple of bottles of champagne to be consumed for family celebrations—not to sell to the public!"

The customs officer smiled.

"So they *are* human after all!" chirped Blundell.

A car took the pair back to Portsmouth, dropped the Commander, and delivered Ouvry to the doorstep of Somerfields at 2130. As he hurried in a small cry came through the upper window. He was home.

13

Concerto for Left Hand

THE War was over. Or almost. A bargeload of German mines—one of many recovered at the Baltic and Continental ports—was rendered safe over on the other side. With primers and detonators out, they were dispatched for disposal of the more important parts to Portsmouth. A routine job. The load reached Pompey, and was conveyed up the harbour near to Frater mine depot—not far from Fareham and the Ouvry home, now rapidly resuming a peace-time trim.

Sub-Lieutenant Wilkinson, with an American officer, started stripping the parts from them early in the morning after arrival. Their actions relapsed into a regular rhythm. Out came the components. Wilkinson's mind was very much on the job, and his hands worked with the precise control of the brilliant pianist, which he was. Through his brain stormed the strains of the Brahms second concerto as oddments came out of the mine and were handed to his colleague. He had the soft, sensitive eyes of the pure musician, and to-day he was thinking much of music. Soon the War would really be over, and he would be going back to it once and for all. To-day, on a gay summer day with the War all but won.

The sun shone.

"Had enough yet?" Wilkinson asked the American.

"Any time you say, chum."

"Well"—looking at his watch—"it's twelve twenty-five, so I vote we get a bite now and resume operations such as they are, in an hour."

"Okay by me."

"I'll just hack through this bunch of leads here, and we'll be able to get the rest of the bits and pieces out when we come back."

At 1321 they were on the job again. What Wilkinson did not know was that by cutting through the leads before lunch he had made an electrical circuit linked to a tiny explosive charge. A clock, set to one hour, had been started which was designed to fire a little charge, and so flood and sink the mine. Normally this would have happened only after a predetermined time-lag. Now the clock had been run by the pair of pliers across its leads.

Wilkinson glanced at his watch once more.

"Not bad going—1322. Under the prescribed hour. Too conscientious, that's the trouble with us!"

He sat astride the mine. It was low and cylindrical—not the spherical kind. He had just got nicely settled when a nasty little crack rent the still air. He toppled off his perch, slightly dazed and hurt. He clutched the base of his spine.

"It's got me here, it seems. Nothing much, though."

The American propped him up beside the wretched mine, got an ambulance along, and escorted him to Haslar, the naval hospital at the entrance to the harbour on the Gosport side. He soon recovered, to all appearances.

Next day he was sitting up in bed.

"Hello, Yank!" He smiled slightly.

"What's happened to your hand, chum?" the American asked agitatedly.

"Something's snapped. I've got no control of my fingers in this right hand." Wilkinson spoke softly, a frown furrowing above his eyes. He could not pretend gaiety.

"Gee, that's tough; but don't you worry a second, Wilky—they'll get it all right in no time. They do wonders these days with chaps far worse than that. Just you remember, see? And don't let it get you down, fellow."

"Thanks."

He watched the American officer walking down the ward. Watched him right out of sight. He had gone. His hand had gone—or might just as well have done.

Wilkinson turned his head slowly away, to see the surgeon coming along from the opposite end of the ward.

"Oh, Wilkinson."

"Yes, sir? What's going to happen, sir?"

"I understand your anxiety, and I'll do all I can, but this is the truth of the matter. I just shan't be able to tell you one way or the other for maybe a year yet. I'm afraid you'll have to resign yourself to a spell of inactivity, away from the piano. I know what it means to you. But there it is. We'll do everything we can. It's not a straightforward case, though, and I can't promise anything. You wanted me to tell you the whole truth, didn't you?"

The Sub nodded. "Thank you, sir. Of course. I appreciate what you've said, and that you've been straight with me. No good beating about the bush. It's just that the piano has meant so much. I'll just have to hope for the best."

"That's the spirit. There's no reason why we shouldn't see an improvement soon. But it's no good trying to rush things."

A year elapsed. Two. But Wilkinson did not get back the use of his fingers. The thumb of the right hand slowly resumed its status, but not the fingers. The nervous system had had a jolt too much for it to stand.

If they had taken their allotted lunch hour that summer's day he would still have been playing with both hands. The clock would have run its course, and the charge gone off harmlessly. He would still know the Brahms, the Emperor, the Schumann—and so much more besides. Wondrous waltzes of Chopin. Fiery passion of Beethoven sonatas. The deep, soul-searing drama of Rachmaninov. All he had left was Ravel. The concerto for left hand.

August 1945. M strode into Ouvry's office. "Looks like the end. We didn't think it would be so soon after VE."

"Yes, it can only be a matter of days now."

"Two things I came in to tell you. I've just had the estimate of enemy ships sunk or seriously damaged by British mines. How many do you think?"

"Difficult to say, really. A thousand, perhaps?"

"Not a bad guess, but the Admiralty figure is no less than 1588. Nearly one a day throughout the War."

"What an amazing achievement!" Ouvry said. "And what a tribute to Mine Design! It's been a real two-way victory. With us in the defence and the minelaying chaps up in the scrum." His heart was still on the rugger-field.

"And while we're on the subject of statistics," M went on, "don't forget the hundreds of specimens Enemy Mining Section has handled. That's without all those washed up on the East Coast which Edwards and his men took care of—and minus the land mines on London. I wonder if people will ever know what you and your little group have really done? Don't ever underestimate it through any false feeling of modesty. It's been quite an epic in its own way, you know."

N

14

War and Peace

WILL-O'-THE-WISP George Gosse, G.C., that elusive Aussie, was destined to turn his bag of an "unsweepable oyster" at Bremen, when clearing the docks and waterways, into a truly remarkable 'double.' But he had to wait nearly ten years to do so—until the Royal Tour of Australia early in 1954.

George was at his home, No. 50 Lefèvre Terrace in North Adelaide, when early one morning the télephone rang. The caller was Commander Cook, Royal Australian Navy, travelling round the country with the entourage of the royal party.

"It's Bill Cook, George."

"Well, well, well. Good to hear from you. What's cooking? No pun intended."

"We've just arrived with the Queen and Duke, and that's why I'm ringing you. I've been vetting the mail, among other duties, and there's a package addressed to Her Majesty that looks more than a little doubtful, and we thought of you at once with that G.C. record of yours! It's been put under the X-ray, and the film shows several oddities. I don't really *think* there's anything lethal about it, but it *could* be a bomb. Would you like to take a look at it, old boy?"

"*Would* I? Just you try and stop me. I can't get

over fast enough. Tell me where you're speaking from."

"Now, wait a minute. You always were the impetuous type. Just stay put and be patient if you can, and I'll send the police out with the thing."

"Lieutenant-Commander Gosse, sir? I'm Detective Whitrod. Commander Cook sent me out here. I expect you know all about it."

"Sure. Come right on in."

"What do you think the best approach is, sir?"

"Well," said Gosse slowly, doffing the jacket he had just donned to answer the door, "well, as the sun's just about as strong as it can be to-day, I suggest a little beer would be the best preliminary, and then we can settle down and take a peep at the picture you got on the old X-ray."

Gosse vanished momentarily, returning with two iced lagers as Whitrod held the black print up for him. Gosse sipped his beer and stared into the plate.

"No doubt about it," he concluded, as the beer-level lowered visibly, "there's a torch-battery of some kind, and a couple of spring clips that look like bicycle-clips. I'd say the other items include a nut and a bolt near one clip, what could be a coil of wire leading to the other, and several shapes that don't seem to mean anything at all."

Gosse also made out silhouettes of an anchor, a banjo, and a bee—all about one and a half to two inches long.

"What does the package itself look like?" Gosse queried.

"I've got it outside in the car. Won't be a second."

Whitrod reappeared with a cardboard box 14 inches by 8 by 2, wrapped up in brown paper, addressed simply:

QUEEN ELIZABETH,
GOVERNMENT HOUSE,
ADELAIDE

It bore twenty-five shillings' worth of airmail stamps and a Melbourne postmark of a couple of days before.

"Can't be much danger in it, whatever else there is," Gosse decided. "A cardboard box is a pretty poor thing to take a booby-trap. And surely no one would send such a parcel by air? All those anchors and oddments seem so out of place, too. It doesn't make sense. I think the arrangement of the clips, wire, and so on is just pure coincidence, although they certainly reminded me of the War, with all those things that look like parts of an electrical circuit. Anyway, let's take it out into the back garden and open it up."

"Nothing doing, I'm afraid, sir." Whitrod remained adamant. "I'll take you down to the Police Barracks if you like, though. What tools do you want?"

"This is really getting rather fantastic!" Gosse smiled. "How the hell can I say? I'll just get a knife and a ball of string."

Behind the barracks they came across a quiet spot and put the package gently on the ground, with a brick on it to keep it still.

"At least it's not ticking," cracked Gosse.

He severed the string round the parcel and cut one end out of the box—without moving it. Both men lowered their heads to see inside.

Crinkled Christmas-paper and cotton-wool confronted them—it was soon after the holiday season—and a plain

lead tube turned out to be glue for making model aero-
planes.

Gosse stuck the knife in the ground, tied the end of
the ball of string to it, wove the string under the box
and over the top, walked away a bit—and pulled.

There was no bang!

They retraced their steps. Anchor, banjo, and bee
became cheap colourful jewellery. The torch battery and
spare bulbs were surrounded by cotton-wool in a little
box, all done up with sticky tape. The "coil of wire,"
which had seemed so mysterious, turned into tinsel
wrapped round a package looking like pencils. Clips and
nut and bolt had been put in just for good measure, and
were not attached to anything!

Gosse and Whitrod stood up and stretched—then
burst out laughing. What was it all about? Gosse
thought it was sent in good faith by some children—
with Mother paying the postage—or else by a simple soul,
trying to express his or her feelings.

"Your guess is as good as mine," he exploded. "Anyway, it was fun while it lasted."

As George Gosse made his way back he was chuckling
to himself. Then he became quiet, contemplative, as he
remembered the more serious specimens they had dealt
with at *Vernon*, in the days of a decade ago. Yet even
then there had been the lighter moments.

His mind flashed from Adelaide. He was bringing
home the bacon to Britain in the form of a Japanese
mine from the east coast of India.

M was telling Ouvry at West Leigh Cottage: "Well,
it's arrived at last, and I hear that it has been marked
'High Explosive. Dangerous. Not to be opened until

Lieutenant Gosse is present.' So he had it very much to himself on the liner coming over. An officer on board has just been telling me that the customs took one look at it, moved several steps smartly to the rear, and passed it through in double-quick time."

"How priceless!"

"Now we're all waiting for Gosse to show up," M continued. "The mine's over at West Leigh House, and the whole scientific section are anxious to see inside."

"I suppose Gosse knew what he was about, putting that notice on it," Ouvry mused. "Still, it does seem a bit strange. It should be all right by now, though. He must have made it safe and sound before crossing half the world in a liner with it."

"You'd certainly think so. Anyway, we'll soon see. He rang me to say he'll be here in a few minutes."

A sentry stood by the mine. A group of scientists, some bearded, others bespectacled, all eager, encircled Gosse as he came on the scene. He looked as cheerful as ever, if a little sheepish—Gosse, with his bold black beard and, behind it, soft brown eyes and a softer-still voice.

Off came the cover-plate. Then the top of the charge-case. Breathlessly the group huddled round as he handled the explosive quite nonchalantly—which turned out to be neat little packages of nylons and perfume!

"Bless my soul!" said Ouvry. "Now I see why you wanted your notice kept on, you old rogue!"

"Couldn't afford customs," Gosse said simply. "Not on my pay. We're not all capitalist commanders, you know."

The last enemy mine had been rendered safe.

Appendix

AWARDS

The awards listed below were given to those engaged in rendering mines safe. The decorations marked thus † were not awarded for this work. The officers and men whose names are marked with an asterisk were killed. It should be stated that the list is not necessarily complete, nor were all the people listed based at *Vernon*.

G. Thistleton-Smith	Commander, R.N.	G.M.
G. B. Sayer	Commander, R.N.	D.S.C.†
E. O. Obbard	Commander, R.N.	D.S.C., G.M.
C. E. Hamond	Commander, R.N.	D.S.O., D.S.C.
J. G. D. Ouvry	Commander, R.N.	D.S.O.
J. E. M. Glenny	Lieut.-Commander, R.N.	D.S.O., D.S.C.
R. C. Lewis	Lieut.-Commander, R.N.	D.S.O., O.B.E.†
*R. B. Edwards	Lieut.-Commander, R.N.	D.S.O.
R. S. Armitage	Lieut.-Commander, R.N.V.R.	G.C., G.M.
G. A. Hodges	Lieut.-Commander, R.N.V.R.	G.M., Dispatches
H. E. Wadsley	Lieut.-Commander, R.N.V.R.	D.S.C., G.M. and Bar
E. O. Gidden	Lieut.-Commander, R.N.V.R.	G.C., O.B.E., G.M.
H. R. Newgass	Lieut.-Commander, R.N.V.R.	G.C.
D. W. Speirs	Lieut.-Commander, R.N.R.	G.M.
M. W. Griffiths	Lieut.-Commander, R.N.V.R.	G.M.
C. W. A. Chapple	Lieut.-Commander, R.N.V.R.	D.S.C.,† G.M.
G. G. Turner	Lieut.-Commander, R.N.V.R.	G.C., G.M.
G. E. Stubbs	Lieut.-Commander, R.N.V.R.	G.M.
L. V. Goldsworthy	Lieut.-Commander, R.A.N.V.R.	G.C., D.S.C., G.M.
J. S. Mould	Lieut.-Commander, R.A.N.V.R.	G.C., G.M.

R. H. Syme	Lieutenant, R.A.N.V.R.	G.C., G.M. and Bar
G. Gosse	Lieutenant, R.A.N.V.R.	G.C.
E. E. Ruttle	Lieutenant, R.A.N.V.R.	M.B.E.
*G. H. Goodman	Lieutenant, R.N.V.R.	G.C., M.B.E.
E. D. Woolley	Lieutenant, R.N.V.R.	G.M. and Bar
E. T. C. Tewson	Lieutenant, R.N.V.R.	G.M.
T. A. Gray	Lieutenant, R.N.V.R.	M.B.E.
M. T. Howard Williams	Lieutenant, R.N.V.R.	M.B.E.
W. R. Nickson	Lieutenant, R.N.V.R.	G.M.
K. J. Townley	Lieutenant, R.N.V.R.	M.B.E.
S. A. Wilkinson	Lieutenant, R.N.V.R.	Dispatches
P. V. Danckwerts	Sub-Lieutenant, R.N.V.R.	G.C.
*R. B. Sutherland	Sub-Lieutenant, R.N.V.R.	Dispatches
*C. E. Baldwin	Chief Petty Officer	D.S.M.
*R. Tawn	Diver Able Seaman	D.S.M.
A. L. Vearncombe	Able Seaman	D.S.M.
Pearson	Able Seaman	G.M.
L. Walden	Mr	G.M.
H. W. W. Kelly	Mr	M.B.E.
A. B. Wood	Dr	O.B.E.